HOW TO MANAGE
PRESSURE BEFORE
PRESSURE MANAGES

You

Other Zondervan Books by Tim LaHaye . . .
How to Win Over Depression
Revelation—Illustrated and Made Plain
Ten Steps to Victory Over Depression
The Act of Marriage (with Beverly LaHaye)
Anger Is a Choice (with Bob Phillips)

HOW TO MANAGE PRESSURE BEFORE PRESSURE MANAGES

You

TIM LaHAYE

ZONDERVAN PUBLISHING HOUSE
of The Zondervan Corporation, Grand Rapids, Michigan

Library of Congress Cataloging in Publication Data
LaHaye, Tim F.
  How to manage pressure before pressure manages you.

    Bibliography: p.
    Includes index.
    1. Stress (Psychology)   2.   Christian life—
1960–   .   I. Title.
BF575.S75L24   1983   248.4   83-10253
ISBN 0-310-27081-2

Printed in the United States of America
83 84 85 86 87 88 / 9 8 7 6 5 4 3 2 1

Contents

Acknowledgments

The following versions of Scripture are used in this book:

✦ *The Holy Bible: The New International Version* (NIV), copyright © 1978 by the New York International Bible Society. Used by permission.

The New American Standard Bible (NASB), copyright © 1960, 1962, 1963, 1968, 1971, 1972, 1973, 1975, 1977 by the Lockman Foundation, La Habra, California. Used by permission.

The New King James Bible, The New Testament (NKJ), copyright © 1979 by Thomas Nelson Inc., Publishers, Nashville, Tennessee.

The King James Version (KJV).

Any Scripture quotations not designated by a specific version are renderings by the author of this book.

The publisher is grateful for permission to use extensive quotations from the following books:

Daniel A. Girdano and George S. Everly, Jr., *Controlling Stress and Tension: A Holistic Approach,* copyright © 1979, pp. 25, 91–92. Reprinted by permission of Prentice-Hall, Inc., Englewood Cliffs, N.J.

Tim LaHaye, *Understanding the Male Temperament,* © 1977 by Tim LaHaye, published by Fleming H. Revell Company, Old Tappan, N.J. Used by permission.

Walter McQuade and Ann Aikman, *Stress,* copyright © 1974 by Walter McQuade and Ann Aikman. Reprinted by permission of the publisher, E. P. Dutton, Inc., New York.

Keith W. Sehnert, *Stress/Unstress,* copyright © 1981 by Augsburg Publishing House, Minneapolis, Minn.

Hans Selye, M.D., *Stress Without Distress* (J. B. Lippincott), copyright © 1974 by Hans Selye, M.D. Abridged specified excerpts reprinted by permission of Harper & Row, Publishers, Inc.

Jere E. Yates, *Managing Stress,* p. 41, copyright © 1979 by AMACOM, a division of American Management Associations, New York, N.Y. All rights reserved.

Preface

Until recently I had decided that being a successful pastor for thirty years, the author of books which had sold six million copies, the founder of ten different organizations, a father and grandfather, a twin-engine pilot, a compulsive jogger, and a speaker with more invitations than I could handle made me exempt from pressure.

Then came television! Within four months of launching a TV show on family life, my wife and I faced the greatest pressures we had ever experienced: Not enough time, too much travel, production deadlines, organizational tensions, frustrated dreams, disappointments by people, and the ever-present, forever-nagging problem of "insufficient funds."

Television is the best way to reach a maximum number of people in the shortest period of time. A recent survey revealed that there are more TV sets in American homes than bathtubs. In fact, "97 percent of all Americans watch two hours of TV daily," Dan Rather reported on the CBS evening news. However, television consumes money almost as fast as the federal government.

I am not unused to walking by faith. I have built churches, raised millions of dollars for missions, and instituted citywide and national campaigns. I certainly am not a fearful person. In 1979 I launched an aggressive attack against the most powerful force for evil in the United States today—secular humanism—

openly criticizing the secular humanist policies of the then president and vice-president of the nation. I debated a UCLA professor at the fortieth annual convention of the American Humanist Association and confronted three liberals in a debate at the largest theological seminary in the country. I have debated former U.S. Sen. Frank Church on "The David Susskind Show," appeared on "The Phil Donahue Show," and agreed to debate TV producer Norman Lear if he would accept. So obviously I have experienced the rigors of pressure.

But the greatest pressure I have known in my life stems from our TV ministry. That is why I felt led to write this book—because I have learned that God is able to give victory amid incredible pressure. He has promised to supply *all* our needs according to His limitless resources.

You face pressure too, don't you? Regardless of your place in the game of life, you will inevitably be confronted with real pressures—and if you don't handle them, they will handle you.

Life itself is a pressure. That's what Eliphaz meant when he said, "Man is born unto trouble [pressure] as the sparks fly upward" (Job 5:7). I can't remove your pressure; only God can do that. But I *can* help you learn to handle your pressures the way God has enabled me to cope with mine.

If reading this book teaches you how to avoid unnecessary pressures and how to deal with those that are inescapable, then my pressures will not have been experienced in vain. If you would like to share your victories with me, I would be pleased to hear from you. Of one thing I am certain: Whatever your pressure, "God meant it for your *good*" —not to sink you or hurt you, but for your benefit.

CHAPTER 1

Pressure Is Inescapable

Pressure is an inevitable part of life. No one is immune to it. In fact, it is as old as man himself. Adam and Eve faced a pressurized decision in the Garden of Eden—and cracked under it. Billions have followed in their footsteps.

This book is not intended to help you escape pressure, for—as we shall see—the strain of circumstance is essential to a normal life. Contrary to popular opinion, pressure is not harmful unless it gets out of control or lasts too long. But it must be managed properly or it can shorten your life and make you miserable.

Two brothers face the same pressures of life. One is a healthy, happy, and highly motivated success. The other is a sickly, pessimistic failure. They were reared in the same environment, attended the same schools, even pursued the same professions. However, one learned to manage his pressures, whereas the other is manipulated by his.

Identical twin sisters, Sarah and Sue, grew up in similar circumstances. Both married devoted husbands, yet the happiest sister endured the heaviest pressures. Sarah, the one with the extra problems, had three children, one of whom was born with a serious physical handicap. At age twenty-nine her husband died. Sue had three healthy children, but allowed her pressures to manage her. She took her own life at thirty-one. Sarah eventually married Sue's husband and became the contented mother of six children. I'll let you decide whether she learned to manage her pressures.

UNEMPLOYMENT

As a guest on "The Phil Donahue Show," I listened to a woman caller describing her husband's disinterest in sex. In questioning her, I found that they had five children and he was unemployed. No wonder he showed signs of impotence. Because to a man unemployment is one of the greatest pressures in life, financial stress may short-circuit a normal sex drive.

Sexual promiscuity can often be traced to employment pressures. Women without strong moral commitment are often pressured into trading sexual favors for job advancement, security, or salary increases. They don't intend to be promiscuous and they are not victims of sexual harassment, but their actions relieve the pressure caused by job insecurity.

By contrast, other women are driven to frigidity by economic pressures. Relaxation is essential to enjoyable sexual expression, but responsible people, both male and female, tend to find their concentration eroded by thoughts of financial pressure.

The first financial strain I can remember confronted me at the age of twelve. I was fired by the *Detroit News* from my job as a newsboy because government bureaucrats decided to pass child labor laws that prohibited children from working until age fourteen. I considered myself a financial failure at twelve! That pressure produced the second major depression in my life. The first had occurred three years earlier when my father died unexpectedly at the age of thirty-four. All life experiences such as these produce pressure that in turn creates stress, tension, and other emotional and physical reactions.

How you cope with these pressures determines the degree of stress they place on you. The only way to reduce the stress is to lighten the pressure. Notice that I didn't say *remove* the pressure, for that may not serve your best interests. But you can learn to manage your pressures before they produce harmful stresses that destroy or shorten your life.

It is idealistic nonsense to strive for a pressure-free life. But it is foolhardy to let your spontaneous pressures create such stress hormones in your body that you ruin your health, emotions, and spirit. No matter how gigantic the pressures, they can be endured.

God has promised that all pressures or "temptations"—sometimes called "trials"—"are common to man, *but* God is faithful! He will not allow you to be tempted beyond what you are able . . . to bear" (1 Cor. 10:13). This is one of the most important verses in the Bible on pressure. In other words, God will *never* let your pressures become so weighty that you will crack under them.

By now you are probably thinking, "Wait a minute, Tim, I know Christians who *have* cracked under pressure." So do I! A few months ago I almost cracked under my own pressures. Does that mean God is *not* faithful? Of course not. We must keep reminding ourselves, in the midst of any pressure, *God is faithful.* He doesn't have to try to be faithful—He just *is.* Just as His nature incorporates holiness and love, it includes faithfulness. There will always be "a way of escape" from the pressures of life, trial, adversity, and temptation. In fact, this verse promises that when necessary, He "will *make* a way of escape."

I find it comforting in my pressure to know three things in advance:

1. God is faithful.
2. Pressure is common to all people.
3. There is a way of escape.

THIS IS PRESSURE!

In 1934, during the Great Depression, my father had been out of work one year. Finally he found a job at the Ford Motor Company in Dearborn, Michigan, and we started to live a normal family life again. I was nine years old and my sister Peggy was five when mom gave birth to my brother Dick. Five weeks later, my father suffered a heart attack and died in two weeks at the age of thirty-four. His $5,000 insurance policy had lapsed for nonpayment thirty days earlier.

At twenty-nine years of age my widowed mother with an eleventh-grade education applied for welfare. But we didn't qualify: We had moved two miles across the county line and had not been residents long enough. Fortunately my parents had accepted Jesus Christ as their Lord and Savior some six years before. When my mother turned to God and laid her dilemma at His feet, He proved incredibly faithful. Oh, He didn't send her a million dollars, but after she prayed for guidance, He led her to a job folding sheets in a hospital laundry for sixty cents an hour. From that "door of escape" she found employment in a factory and eventually learned the trade of drawing electronic wire through diamond dies.

My mother's "door" was not an easy one. In fact, it was marked by work, work, and more work. God doesn't seem to do for us what we can do for ourselves, but He keeps His promises. If we seek Him and His kingdom first, He always supplies our needs. During those next eighteen years she not only raised all three of us to serve God, but taught us how to live and how to work for a living. We are all "workaholics"—and love it.

Besides advancing professionally, she put herself through night school at the Detroit Bible College. When my brother graduated from high school and entered the air force, she resigned a high-paying job—$13,000 annually for a woman employee in 1946 was big money!—to become the director of Child Evangelism Fellowship in Lansing, Michigan. For twenty-three years she held one of the largest Child Evangelism ministries in the country; led thousands of boys and girls, young people, and their parents to Christ; and trained many CEF workers, some of whom today are directors of their own CEF clubs.

Her life was never free of pressure—and neither is yours. But she was not overcome by her pressures—though I imagine she was human enough to feel overwhelmed at times, and so it will be with you.

You cannot avoid the pressures of life, but you can certainly whittle them down to size and trust God to see you through them. If you don't, they will occasion severe distress and possible shorten your life.

No one likes pressure. Even the most choleric individual recoils from pressure some of the time. Although he relishes confrontation and venturesome challenge, he needs to relax at times; since he seldom does, he endures a high mortality rate. Relaxation through a life of trust in the Lord will lengthen his life.

CHAPTER 2

Every Stage of Life
Has Its Peculiar Pressures

Pressure originates with the activities of life. Like God, it is no respecter of persons. Usually the pressure builds in direct proportion to the degree of change in a situation. For example, the Little Leaguer is excited and pressured in his first time at bat. After a while the pressure subsides and the enjoyment increases. However, when he tries out for the high school baseball team, the pressure returns his first time up; then it is gradually alleviated as he "gets used to" that level of sports. No matter how good an athlete he may be, he will face that cycle each time he moves up the changing ladder of success, from college ball to the minor leagues to the majors and perhaps the World Series. "It's fun," he reminds himself—but there is still pressure.

Remember the first time you drove a car? Pure panic! Now you shift gears, park, and edge into traffic without really thinking. I will never forget the first time I pushed in the throttle of an airplane. I was panic-stricken. Then one day the instructor climbed out, and I sat at the end of the runway all by myself. Talk about pressure! The stress hormones activated by my system irrigated every sweat gland in my body. My mind was excitingly clear, but my heart was in my throat, and fear almost prevented me from trying something I had wanted to do since boyhood. Now, hundreds of hours later, I can honestly say that I find flying relaxing—as long as the engine stays lit.

So it is with life. We can't avoid change, and change produces pressure. The greater the change, the greater the pressure.

"Misery likes company," the saying goes. If that is true, it should be comforting to know that no one is immune to pressure. If you identify the age, sex, stage in life, or kind of change, I can suggest an acute pressure—and life can suggest hundreds of others. As we shall see, change is not the only ingredient that generates pressure, but it is the most common one. Consider four stages of life.

CHILDHOOD PRESSURES

From potty training to graduation, children feel pressure. In fact, many doctors suggest that the process begins at the moment of birth. When a child leaves the warmth of the dark, watery insulator of his mother's womb and ventures into the sterile environment, bright lights, and seventy-degree temperatures of a hospital room, life becomes pressured. No wonder he screams. The noted French doctor Frederick Leboyer suggests that the infant's experience is less traumatic if he is born in a dark, warm room and placed immediately on his mother's stomach.

Every child needs "the elasticity of youth" to cope with the pressure of learning, learning, learning. First there is learning to crawl, then to talk, walk, run, read, write, and recite those wretched math tables. Some parents unwisely place enormous pressures on their children by demanding that they be first in everything.

All children have inherited a temperament combination from their parents that determines, among other things, their learning speed. Sanguine children are quick learners (and sometimes easy forgetters) in the curious search for new things. Eagerly delving into everything, they seem bright from the first day. The choleric aggressive child, who is curious, will take everything apart and destroy anything not made of steel. The melancholy child, normally less venturesome, is a deep thinker. He usually knows much more than his parents realize because, not being an extrovert, he doesn't speak out. The calm, contented phlegmatic child may be so unmotivated that he lives in

a dream world. Such children need their curiosity levels stimulated. Naturally the combination of temperaments will influence them also. (A fuller presentation of temperament and
its influences on behavior will be provided in chapter 7.)

It is important that you understand your child's temperament and work with it. Encourage, teach, and lead him. This is
the primary role of parenting.

Even after a child goes to school, he faces pressure: Bicycle
riding, roller-skating, sports, self-discipline, social adjustment,
peer acceptance, and identification with authority figures. Ultimately he comes to the delightful experience of being confronted with the pressures of the opposite sex. If his parents are
"nomads" who move frequently, his pressures are magnified
because the frequency and degree of changes in his life increase.

At this stage in life, home should be his haven. It need not
be a palace to have a positive influence on a child's character
and upbringing. However, it must serve as a sanctuary where
he feels comfortable, relaxed, and welcome—even though he
must conform to rules and guidelines. He must learn to obey
authority sometime in life, so it might as well be in the haven
where he is loved best. All children need a place where they can
relax and confidently expect the safety and basic creature comforts that home provides.

Recently a mother shared her goals for her son. As the
result of his work and efforts by his parents, he was "finally
becoming a good reader. If I can get him into a strong summer
school program, he will be ahead of his grade level for second
grade." Pressure, pressure, pressure—at 7 years of age! It is no
wonder that many children are suffering from educational
burnout by the time they reach the fourth grade.

Young children do not need the performance pressures im-
posed on them by well-meaning adults; they require love, security, and acceptance. And they should be assured that at any
time they can run into the hearts of the adults most important
on the earth to them—their parents. There will be plenty of
time for the pressures of learning. Childhood should be a carefree period of life when the emphasis is more on character
building than on academic attainment.

TEENAGE PRESSURES

The teen years should form the happiest period of a person's life. However, the rate of teenage suicide suggests that the reverse is true at present. "Self-inflicted death has increased fourfold among our nation's youth," states one authority. "Suicide is the leading cause of death among persons between the ages of 13 and 19, and the rate is rising among children as young as 6 years of age."[1] Obviously something must be wrong.

At a time when their motor skills may not give them control over their own rapidly growing bodies, teenagers are forced to compete with other teens two or more years their senior. In fact, leaving elementary school for seventh grade can be very traumatic, for students are forced to say farewell to their secure world, where sixth graders are positioned on the top rung, and start over on the bottom of the junior high school ladder. Add to this an awakening sex drive with new and uncertain passions, and you can begin to appreciate some of the pressures that contribute to seventh-grader insecurities.

Have you considered the incredible pressures our young people face today? In a five-to-eight-year period of time they will be forced to make decisions about learning, vocation, morality, and life itself. Where they go to college, whom they will marry, where they will live and work—all are life-molding decisions.

Just four years ago their parents were the most powerful influence in their lives. Today it is their peer group, made up of other equally insecure, inexperienced young people—probably more rebellious than any similar group in the history of the world. The power of peer pressure on youth becomes apparent in their attire, speech, and habits.

To make matters worse, teens are confronted with the unprecedented pressures of alcohol, marijuana, pornography, and the everpresent temptations to sexual activity long before they are old enough to bear the responsibility for such actions. A

---

[1]Barbara M. Morris, *Change Agents in the Schools* (Ellicott City, Md.: The Barbara M. Morris Report, 1979), p. 174.

concerned mother recently informed me of the discovery of a letter, in the desk of her thirteen-year-old son, from a fourteen-year-old schoolmate who was propositioning him to take her to bed. If ever our teens needed to be well indoctrinated in traditional moral values, it is today!

The pressure of group conformity has reached unbelievable proportions. *Time* magazine recently pointed out that after a generation of sex education and millions of dollars spent on dispensing contraceptive information and devices through Planned Parenthood (often without parental consent), more than one million unwed teens will get pregnant this year. And most will get pregnant deliberately! Some "want something to love," others think it will make their boyfriends love them, and many get pregnant just because it is "the 'in' thing."

TEENAGE REBELLION INCREASES

Ours is an age of rebellion. The humanistic psychologists of the past have brainwashed an entire generation of parents with the false notion that permissiveness is the way to raise children. Drawing on French skeptic Jean Jacques Rousseau's well-advertised fallacy that human nature is perfectible and that, if left to themselves, children would make the right choices in life, humanists have produced a generation of rebels. Indulged from birth, young people possess little self-control or self-discipline, and consequently they are unable to absorb the frustrations and pressures of life. All too frequently we read bizarre illustrations of teenage rebellion, from excessive sibling rivalry to murder of parents. Extreme? Yes, but increasing at an alarming rate.

Unfortunately anger and hostility impair good judgment, and bad decisions only seem to compound the pressures of life. Solomon exhorted us, "Foolishness is bound up in the heart of a child, but the rod of instruction will drive it far from him" (Prov. 22:15). A rebel is usually estranged from the very people who can counsel him best at those times in life when he needs the advice of sane judgment. He often looks to his peers for guidance instead, but they are frequently as rebellious as he. As a result, the rebel subjects himself to the increasing pressures of life and fails to locate the pathway of happiness. According to the psalmist, "Blessed [happy] is the man who does not walk in the counsel of the ungodly, or stand in the way of sinners, or sit in the seat of the scornful [another term for rebellion]" (Ps. 1:1). Truly, "the way of the transgressor is hard."

COMMITTED TEENS FACE PRESSURE TOO

I have worked with young people long enough to know that the old axiom "All young people are going to the dogs" is not true. The high school youth in my own church and Christian school as well as the dedicated students I have addressed at Christian colleges throughout the nation convince me that the church has an army of committed and capable young leaders preparing for the years ahead. I feel good about the future.

However, these committed youth—particularly those who attend public schools—are facing far greater peer pressure than their parents did at a comparable age. Only by purposing in their hearts, like Daniel of old, not to contaminate their minds or morals with the fleshpots of their society have they made it into young adulthood. But it hasn't been easy. And this may be the key to their present strength: They came through the fires of teenage pressure and have built up inner endurance. Like others before them, they are discovering that the fight is worth it. Unfortunately many young people have cracked under the pressure and in some cases will bear the scars for life.

TEENAGE RESOURCES

A generation ago our culture supported the moral values taught in the home. Thanks to the secular humanists who control our public schools, media, government, and courts, this is no longer true. Today the living conditions of Sodom and Gomorrah surround us. This is why the home, the church, and the Christian school are so important in the lives of our teenagers.

Strong young people are usually products of strong families. Dedicated parents, I have observed, are gradually awakening to the realization that they must spend more quality time with their children to prepare them for life. It takes time to communicate love, values, and a philosophy of life. Two generations ago most young people usually had to work with their parents on the farm or at home just to survive economically. Today, between our affluence and the complexity of modern technology, this is no longer necessary or even possible. How can the son of a doctor, dentist, lawyer, teacher, or minister assist his father during his working day? The time they share must take place at home after working hours. And that is my point. Seldom do we naturally find time to do things together anymore; we have to *make* it. If you have children or teens in your home, check your priority list. If their names do not appear near the top in your time allotment, you had better recheck your lifestyle.

James C. Dobson, the highly respected child psychologist, tells the delightful story of his father's investment in his life, teaching him to excel at tennis. Dr. Dobson stresses the importance of self-acceptance: Everyone must learn to do something well. His father spent several years trying to teach young Jim to play tennis; never once did Jim beat his father. One day when Jim was in the ninth grade, a high school senior challenged him to a game. To his amazement, Jim was victorious. This was the first time he recognized his outstanding ability as a ninth-grade tennis player. The discovery did wonders for his self-confidence and self-image. Father Power is a tremendous resource—when utilized.

One of the many family policies that can really fortify young people in these morally corruptive days is regular training in the Word of God. Whether labeled family devotions, family Bible study, or family worship, it should be a time, four or more days a week, when the family gathers around the Word of God to read, pray, praise, and sing. It need not consume a lot of time, but when done sincerely, it can give support and direction to these young, unguided missiles through mighty stormy days.

Another powerful resource is Scripture memorization as a family. During the last three years of my church pastoral ministry, I encouraged our entire church family to memorize at least one verse a week (a verse that appeared in the church bulletin). Hundreds of verses were stored away along with their subject headings and references. Such a practice enables family members to endure the pressures of life by helping them to make the right decisions. The Bible says, "Your Word have I hid in my heart, that I might not sin against you" (Ps. 119:11).

The church is another powerful resource for developing teens in a decaying society. However, it must be a Bible-teaching church that demonstrates a vital concern for today's young people. It not only provides a qualitative peer group in which to grow up but offers programs, principles, and challenges to a committed life at a crucial time. With dismay I have watched soft-hearted parents heed the transitory cry of a teen to drop out of the Christian youth group—and live to regret it. Don't be surprised if outside pressures at times cause your teenager to yearn for the fleshpots of Egypt, Los Angeles, Detroit, or Dallas. That's the time they need the countervailing force of parental pressure to keep them on the right track. Don't be afraid to apply it—but do it in love.

A summer Christian camp experience is a powerful resource to a teenager plagued with the pressures of modern living. Not only is it a time to get away from home and meet other young people his age, but it also provides a vital opportunity to issue a concentrated challenge regarding commitment to the cause of Christ. As we shall see, one can ease pressure by investing his life, including his goals and vision, in something greater than himself. The high school or college youth with a vision is much better equipped to face youthful pressures than one who floats aimlessly down the river of life, usually running aground or sinking altogether.

Since many who read this book are raising a teen (or will do so one day), let me challenge you to prayerfully envision sending your young person to "Bible school" after he finishes high school. Regardless of his vocation, one or more years in a Bible school will enrich his life. In fact, as a layman in his church, whether a laborer or professional person, he will be equipped by this for a lifetime of Christian service. If he does not plan to attend a good Christian college, nine months in a Bible school will prove invaluable in preparing him to cope with the pressures of life and enabling him to become a prepared "workman" in the kingdom of God as he earns his living—no matter what his living is.

I feel strongly about the issue of spiritual preparation, because of my decisions as a youth. Knowing that I would spend my nineteenth and twentieth years in the United States Army Air Forces, I decided in the eleventh grade to add a few evening classes so I could graduate in January of my senior year. At age 17½ I spent four months at Moody Bible Institute in Chicago, which equipped me for the pressure of army life in the U.S. and one year in Europe. Many times I have thanked God for that one semester at Moody Bible Institute.

If I were a camp director today, I would establish a Bible institute program every year from February through May for young people who have been subjected to a steady diet of humanism in the public schools. Such biblical teaching would significantly help to prepare them for the next major stage in their lives. Because the senior year in many high schools is largely "fun and games," Christian young people should be able to work a program of serious biblical studies into their schedules. An effective Bible institute program, reaching and developing lives over several years, would result in a tremendous increase in Christian workers and leaders throughout the Christian community.

EVEN NEWLYWEDS FACE PRESSURE

One would think that newlyweds would be the happiest, most unpressured people on earth. However, on a pressure scale of 1 to 100, the act of getting married totals 50 points. If problems erupt during the "adjustment period" (the first three years), the score can go significantly higher.

The most common source of pressure for newlyweds is finances. The cost of living tends to be highest when we begin our post-high school lives and our skills (potential for income) are in least demand. It is a rare high school graduate who is worth minimum wage until his on-the-job training is complete. In fact, many college graduates do not earn their pay for months after they commence working. Instituting a home today is essentially the same for everyone: Housing, food, transportation, and almost every other cost do not vary widely. Thus most couples begin a marriage with both members working.

It is essential that newly marrieds plan a budget carefully and avoid the modern Slough of Despond: Credit buying. The credit card is one of the worst inventions of mankind; it leads to overspending and the tyranny of financial pressure. One survey we took of divorced couples indicated that sixty-one out of one hundred broken homes were split by financial problems. Even when they do not lead to divorce, financial difficulties place undue pressure on a marriage. Here is a good rule to follow: Never go into debt for anything that cannot be sold for more money than is borrowed against it. This principle will allow one to purchase a home or car, if sufficient equity is raised for a down payment. In most other cases you will reduce pressure down to size by paying cash. If you cannot pay cash, wait.

Here is another financial policy for people in general and newlyweds in particular: Enjoy God's blessing on your financial affairs by giving one-tenth of all that you earn to Him. I learned this from my widowed mother, who amassed her earnings at the rate of sixty cents an hour. A concerned relative told her, "Margaret, God doesn't expect a widow woman with three small children to tithe." Fortunately my mother did not heed that advice. God blessed the fifty-four-cents-an-hour income that remained after she gave the first six cents to Him; we never went hungry, we always had sufficient clothing to wear, and all our basic needs were supplied. I have never known an exception to this divine principle. The Scripture promises, "Honor the Lord with your wealth, with the firstfruits of all your crops; then your barns will be filled to overflowing" (Prov. 3:9–10).

SEXUAL PRESSURES

Another pressure unique to newlyweds involves sexual difficulties. The sex drive in human beings is so powerful that it is ignored at one's own peril. This is why my wife and I wrote *The Act of Marriage:* To provide the Christian community with a Bible-based manual on sexual relations in marriage that is both wholesome and scientific. That it has supplied a need is evidenced by the 1.3 million copies that are now in print and the thousands of responses that have commended its helpfulness. God's beautifully designed means of reducing sexual pressures is called marriage.

Generally speaking, the couple who do not learn through the art of lovemaking the joys of mutual orgasmic expression build up pressure in their relationship. However, just being married does not always resolve sexual pressure. Because many couples do not learn the art of lovemaking, one or both partners may not experience the satisfying orgasm God has designed for them.

This beneficial means of mutual release for sexual tensions in both the husband and wife was intended as a unifying force in their relationship. However, if difficulties arise in this matter and one or both are frustrated instead of satisfied, pressure mounts.

The ideal time to resolve this pressure is shortly after marriage. This is probably one reason why new husbands in the Old Testament were exempt from military service for the first year after their wedding. Couples who find it difficult to discuss their sexual relationship freely usually do not have a satisfying love life. If you need assistance in this matter, I recommend that you read *The Act of Marriage* and discover the key to sexual fulfillment.

MALE AND FEMALE ROLES

One modern factor that creates enormous pressure among newlyweds is a confusion about or a rejection of God's pattern for roles. The biblical teaching that God made Adam and Eve "male and female" confirms that they are two distinctly different persons. This is true not only physically, but mentally and emotionally. In recent years the humanists and feminists have emphasized a merging of the sexes in their campaign for "equality." While one can appreciate the sincere individual who campaigns for sexual equality in the face of discrimination, we cannot change the facts of nature or the design of the Creator. What seems to be missing in this trend is the understanding that two people can be equal but different. More sane heads are beginning to accept the fact that differences do indeed exist between the sexes because God designed them for equal but different purposes.

The biblical pattern has always established the husband as the provider, protector, and leader while the wife is principally equipped to be the homemaker, mother, and partner. This does not preclude the wife from assisting the husband by working

for a time outside the home, as in the case of the woman of
Proverbs 31. Nor does it prevent the husband from assisting
with household chores to make up for the wife's hours spent at
work. In fact, one of the common causes of pressure in the
modern home where both spouses work is the inconsiderate
husband who demands that his wife serve as waitress, cook,
and slave at home.

Even more dangerous is the situation in which the wife
becomes the principal wage-earner. This unscriptural role will
quickly create undue pressure on the relationship, depending
on the couple's temperaments, background, and spiritual vital-
ity.

A man is not prepared to handle female dominance in the
home. It is difficult enough for him to submit to it in the workplace, but at home it destroys his manhood. And if a man is not
a man to himself, he is not a man. Someone has sagely observed, "It is not so important what you are, but supremely
important what you *think* you are."

Man was made to lead, particularly in the home. But a
major dilemma arises when the wife is a more natural leader
than the husband. The more she organizes and presides, the
more he retreats. She may think that he agrees with her leadership, but he will resent her silently until there is nothing left of
their relationship.

A telephone company executive working sixty-five hours a
week was putting a serious strain on his marriage. His strong-
willed wife called the employer and stringently demanded to
know why her husband spent twenty-five additional hours a
week at work for which he was not paid (he was on salary).
Even the boss did not know. Finally the reason surfaced: He
was a leader, but no match for her. Subconsciously he enjoyed
the leadership role at work more than his servant role at home,
so he naturally spent more of his time at work.

A doctor with a beautiful wife at home committed adultery
several times with a "plain Jane" patient. As I delved into the
problem, the solution became apparent. His wife's domineering ways turned the doctor off sexually. With the plain woman
he functioned as a leader. The wife who dominates her husband
at home does so at her own peril.

As a pastoral counselor I get feedback from many of those who have sought help. When I resigned my pastorate after twenty-five years, I received many expressions of love and farewell, not a few from strong-willed wives who had learned the art of female submission. Their initial struggles had been painful, but today they enjoy the love of a good man because they were willing to accept God's role for their lives. Admittedly this requires an act of faith on the wife's part, but it pays off in rich dividends for years to come.

THE HUSBAND'S PART

The same Book that demands wifely submission in an age of feminism also commands the husband to be the loving leader to his wife, using Jesus Christ as the supreme example. In fact, four times Scripture commands the husband to "love his wife." I am convinced that a woman needs love more than anything else in this world. Sex has its place in a sound marriage—on the basis of two or more times a week, depending on age—but a woman's love need goes deeper than this. She wants to be loved as a person. Real love shows itself in actions saturated with kindness, patience, consideration, honor, and the other characteristics of 1 Corinthians 13:4–8.

Nothing builds greater pressure in a woman than the lack of love, particularly by her husband and children. The man who accepts his role as lover and spends sufficient time demonstrating it to the woman he has chosen as his wife will enjoy the undying reward of a lifetime of love, loyalty, and companionship. Who could ask for more out of life?

PARENTS FACE PRESSURES TOO

Twenty to twenty-five years of life is usually spent rearing children. Parenting really isn't very difficult if one makes it a major priority during the early years. However, do not neglect the companionship love with your mate during those same years; otherwise, you may eventually discover that your children have graduated from your home and you have flunked marriage. It is a matter of balance. Ask God to make you an adequate partner while at the same time requesting His help to be an adequate parent. Such balance requires some sacrifices, but you will find that in the long run they are worth it.

The most enriching experience in the world is to rear children who return your love and make something worthwhile of their lives. They don't have to be rich or famous, but they must be productive.

At our Family Life Seminars, my wife and I have often stressed, "You have no more valuable possession in life than your children." That's why we still live in San Diego. Now that we have left the church, we are traveling about three-fourths of the time, to the extent of nearly a quarter-million miles a year. It would make much more sense for us to live in Dallas, the center of the country. We love that city and have many close friends there. But we fly back and forth across the nation week after week because our children and six grandchildren live in San Diego.

Truly, children are "a heritage of the Lord. *Happy* is the man whose quiver is full of them" (Ps. 127:5). And this is one reason Beverly and I—through Concerned Women of America, our weekly television show on family life, and our other pro-family, pro-American activities—are fighting with all our might the humanistic bureaucrats in government who are trying to usurp the role of parents. Children are a heritage of the Lord to parents—not government. They are a blessing to parents—not government.

You may be aware that many Christian families have seen their children taken from them in the name of "child abuse" for little more than spanking them, forbidding them to attend a dance, or refusing to let them associate with certain peers. Some stories in our files would astonish you. When some secular humanist bureaucrat uses the power of government to persecute families, it means that the moral and legal standards in this country have been perverted. This is why we all need to work diligently to elect officials in all positions of government who understand that the laws of this country should be based on the Judeo-Christian moral values of the Bible, not the changing standards of man. Government should be a friend of families, not an antagonist.

All this suggests that parenting demands higher priority

today than it did in previous generations. However, I want young couples and those who contemplate having more children to understand that the current dangers of secular humanism and its corrupting influence on our society do not offer an acceptable excuse for refraining from having children. Remember, conditions were more chaotic and threatening in the first century than now. Those Christian parents suffered pressure from Rome, Nero, and the Jews. Many were thrown to the lions, yet they raised up a generation of evangelists who turned the world upside down in three centuries (as I think we are going to do in this country before the twenty-first century). I am committed, with God's power and the help of millions of Christians in this country, to turn over to my grandchildren a better culture than I inherited. My culture was so strong that a woman could walk the streets late at night without fear of molestation or violence. We all yearn for a return to that kind of civilized culture.

Having said all this, we still must be realistic about the enormous pressures parents face today. According to *U.S. News and World Report,* a typical person works from January 1 to May 10 just to pay his taxes. This amounts to 43 percent of his income. Another 8–12 percent evaporates through inflation, caused by the federal government's spending more than it takes in, forcing it to increase the money supply by printing more money and thereby making our take-home pay worth 8 to 12 percent less.

Money problems are great today. Some economists estimate that it will soon cost more than $25,000 to raise a child through high school. And you will face more than financial pressures in raising him. But don't get discouraged if you feel inadequate for the task. Most parents do. The only parental experts I know are grandparents! Many times you will feel pressure because the activities of life seem out of control. Being confined to a house with little children creates great pressure, ranging from discontent with daily drudgery to unfulfilled dreams. This is particularly true of the college-trained or vocationally experienced woman. She loves and enjoys her children, but longs for the productive routine she once knew.

Be aware of this maxim: Parenting is a temporary trial that

equips a person for other activities later in life. The pressures you face will enrich your character if you do not capitulate to them. We hear a great deal about "burnout" today. Spending fifteen to twenty-five years in the same vocation tends to cause "work burnout." Many women burnouts of age forty or fifty skipped motherhood, but now they are getting tired of their nine-to-five routine. I read recently that career women thirty-three to thirty-eight years old are hastening to have children before they lose the opportunity.

If you are in your early years of parenting, why not relax and enjoy them? Don't allow the pressure of "careeritis" to spoil your present experience. Thank God regularly for your children and give yourself to them. There will be time for a career later—and you will avoid some of the problems of vocational burnout. Besides, a woman who has successfully reared children has more to offer the business world than she realizes. She can take the self-discipline and flexibility that she has learned at home into the workplace. After the new career woman sharpens her skills (which usually doesn't take long), the successful graduate from motherhood makes a better secretary, executive, or worker than she would be otherwise. Just because so many feminists minimize the role of motherhood does not mean that it is not a vital and meaningful vocation. Enjoy it!

Fathers face parental pressures of discipline, training, scheduling time for Little League, etc.—but look on these as an investment in a future adult who will one day be doing the same thing for your grandchildren. The most important ingredient in reducing parental pressure is mental attitude. Enjoy parenthood: It won't last as long as you think.

PARENTS OF TEENS EXPERIENCE UNIQUE PRESSURES

Being the parent of small children can be one of life's most rewarding experiences; parenting teenagers can be nothing less than exciting. Teens can be both amusing and exasperating within a thirty-minute span of time. One moment they act like children; the next moment they behave (or want to) like adults. They often demand adult privileges without the responsibilities. No period can produce more pressure for both the parent and the teenager himself than adolescence.

Our culture offers little help in this regard. Teens are beset by severe temptations, from sex and alcohol to drugs and violence, and the public schools provide little assistance. Whereas a generation ago parents could expect their young people to be challenged academically, learning the skills they will later need to earn a living, this is no longer the case. Their major interests today may be diluted through massive doses of explicit sex education without benefit of moral values. As I have clarified in other books, this irresponsible usurping of parental rights by liberal humanist educators is like pouring emotional gasoline on flickering youthful pressures. Some schools have introduced values clarification, which in my studied opinion is the most devilish attack on traditional moral values yet devised. Add to this courses in death and dying, drug education, psychodrama, and global education, and one concludes that half the curriculum is designed to create conflict at home between student and parent. This produces enormous family pressure.[2] No wonder former U.S. Sen. S. I. Hayakawa, a college president for fifteen years, lamented that "our public schools have educated an entire generation of school children without benefit of moral values."

Add to this the pressure generated by indiscriminate watching of television. Teen are naturally curious; don't be surprised if your youngster wants to emulate his friends, who watch their favorite "stars" regardless of how antimoral and degrading their personal lives or the program content may be.

The parent who has the courage to turn off the TV set faces pressure. If he leaves it on, he will contend with even greater pressure. The next time incest, homosexuality, permissiveness, adultery, and other evils are bootlegged into your home in the guise of humor, and you decide to turn the knob in the middle of the program, it will create pressure!

Generations ago, secular humanists convinced morally minded people that nudity and immorality are acceptable in art and the theater. Now they are doing the same with TV—only this time it invades the home, where each family is faced with

---

[2]See my book *The Battle For the Public Schools* (Old Tappan, N.J.: Fleming H. Revell, 1982).

the responsibility of stopping it. Whether parents shut it off or leave it on, the tube will create pressure unless they have really indoctrinated their children in early life with a deep commitment to biblical moral values.

One other teen-parent pressure cooker involves rock music. Teens often love it, parents hate it, and the naive have no opinion. On one of our recent TV shows, Rev. Dan Peters, an expert on the effects of rock music on the home, pointed out that most parents who object to their teens listening to it do so because of the beat. By contrast, he considered the lyrics and the degenerate lives of the performers even more detrimental. He noted that some rock albums played backward contain a satanic message; I found this hard to believe until I heard it for myself.

Do you understand why you must develop a close, loving relationship with your teen when he is facing these pressures? Interestingly, permissiveness and lack of direction will increase the pressure, not ease it. As we shall see, a major factor in handling pressure is to establish clearly defined guidelines and *stick to them.* At no time in life is it more important that you get a firm grip on your well-advertised guidelines, for your teen will test every rule; if you relent, you will flunk his test and lose credibility. It is better to modify a guideline than relinquish it.

Remember this about teens: They want you to pass their test. They lose respect for the parent who cracks under their pressure. It may sound incongruous, but you are the most stabilizing influence in their lives. If you succumb to their pressure, it will shatter their confidence.

Parents of teens often forget that the most important lesson a child learns at home is obedience. In fact, only two commands in Scripture pertain specifically to children: "Honor and obey your parents." The parent who does not lovingly constrain his teen to obey him will live to regret his weakness. Character is never built by self-indulgence. The adult who was exposed to parental discipline flavored with love as a youth will always make the transition to self-discipline more readily than if he were raised by permissiveness. Do not forget that success is ultimately rooted in self-discipline.

WHAT ABOUT DATING?

Dating, a part of most teenagers' lives, can become the greatest pressure of all. But it need not be so. If parents approach dating unprepared, however, it can create enormous pressure in their hearts. You do not need the added pressure of walking the floor at midnight, wondering where your twelfth-grade son or daughter is.

I learned from my widowed mother that as long as I lived under the same roof, I had to abide by her rules. I wasn't particularly fond of that idea, but I obeyed; I had no options. I am thankful for that today. Had she been more lenient, I probably would have "gone to the dogs."

As our children were approaching the dating stage in life, my involvement in youth camps and conferences led me to believe that most of the conflict between Christian teenagers and their parents arose because no guidelines for dating had been established.

Too often parents decide, "I can trust my children," so they let them establish their own dating standards or give them too much flexibility. Although in some cases this has worked satisfactorily, in many others we have seen the good training of early childhood and adolescence tragically marred by indulgent freedom in the later teen years. Such parents have forgotten the powerful influence teenagers have on each other and the tidal waves of libido that strike all normal young people. It is tragic when the self-control lessons of childhood are overpowerd by these new and exciting drives when teens are least able to cope with them.

In all of life, these teen years offer the greatest emotional instability. It is easy to make decisions on the basis of emotion rather than mind and will. Someone has said, "When the emotion and will are in conflict, the emotions invariably win." This is dangerous, because emotionally made decisions are almost always wrong. It takes a good deal of maturity for any person to learn that only when the mind and emotions agree is it right to proceed with anything. Even then the mind should be guided by the Word of God. Solomon said, "A wise son makes a father glad, but a foolish son is a grief to his mother" (Prov. 10:1), NASB). This is also true of a daughter.

Whenever you have to be inflexible in the application of a rule, bend over backward to be loving and understanding while enforcing it. But don't be too lenient. The United States is the crime leader of the world partly because our judges and our courts do not enforce the laws. Making the same mistake with your teens will not only unnecessarily intensify the pressures of your home, but potentially ruin your teens' lives.

WHAT ABOUT FRIENDS?

Dating is not the only source of pressure-producing conflict in the home. First Corinthians 15:33 warns that "evil company corrupts good morals." Several verses in Scripture teach that the conduct of companions is contagious. Therefore you need to involve yourself in your teenager's company. I have observed that it is easier for one bad apple to spoil a whole barrel than it is for a whole barrel to influence one bad apple.

The turning point of my teen years came when my mother insisted that I break the relationship with my school friends. For five years we had experienced everything together: Sports, school, female friendships, recreation. Now she wanted me to associate with those church kids instead! My mother didn't believe in family voting. Accordingly I changed my friends. As I look back I see that her way was best; but I didn't agree with it then. It created a severe strain at the time, but her action also spared both of us an abundance of pressure and heartache later. Sometimes life's pressure spots are like boils: They are best faced when we temporarily apply more pressure.

SINGLES FACE PRESSURE

The number of singles in our society is mushrooming. Some are divorced, others have delayed marriage, and still others choose to remain single. Because it is a phenomenon that most churches are not equipped to handle, they often hurt people with their unique brand of pressure. The single life may look like a casual, carefree lifestyle on TV, but in the real world it is often subject to intense pressure.

In the counseling room singles talk most about "loneliness." It is no coincidence that loneliness has increased in our society in direct proportion to the expansion of the singles population. Human beings have a great need for companionship, as suggested in Genesis 2. When God saw that there was no "helpmate" for man—no companion—his next creative act fashioned woman.

Although everyone needs a degree of solitude, too much can make one a hermit. To many this prospect is not only pressure-producing but frightening, particularly to a woman. With 9 percent more women in our population than men and in a culture where men initiate most social contacts, it can be frightening to a normal single woman to realize that she may never marry and have children.

If she is not career-minded, but yearns for family, home, and children, she may have to accept her lot: Single for life under duress. With God's help she can do it, but realistically she must acknowledge the accompanying pressures.

The rising crime rate complicates life for singles. They have higher death rates and are involved in more criminal assaults. What single woman does not recognize her vulnerability to the rapist who walks the streets? Personal safety creates its own brand of pressures today, and unless we return to our biblical basis of law, this pressure probably will escalate.

It is frequently more difficult for singles than for married people to make important life decisions, because they have no intimate friends with whom to discuss the details. A divorce may engender unnecessary guilt pressure in the partner who was rejected. As I explain in another book, rejection by a love object is one of the most prevalent triggers of depression.[3] Rejection is naturally followed by self-pity, which always leads to depression. Only by the grace of God can a person undergo severe rejection and rejoice—which is the only key to avoiding depression under those circumstances.

Last year I had to travel alone for several days and arrived at the Amfact Hotel in Dallas. It is a lovely hotel, and Beverly and I have stayed there frequently. But that night I was lonely. I

---

[3]*How to Win Over Depression* (Grand Rapids: Zondervan, 1974).

didn't like the room, the food—anything. When Beverly arrived the next day, my mood was transformed within minutes. That night I began to realize how much I liked the same room, the same food, and the same hotel. The only change was Beverly's arrival. Suddenly I began to appreciate what life must be like for singles, divorcees, and widows. (More than 20 percent of our adult population live alone.) Ever since then I have tried to go out of my way to befriend such people. "God's grace is sufficient" for them, but you and I can help too.

WHAT ABOUT SEX FOR SINGLES?

Sexual pressure is not something that turns on when we get married. Otherwise I fear that more than half the population would be single. Rather, God gave us sexual pressure to speed up the mating process; it is our culture that warps it.

At a recent seminar someone asked, "Is it all right for Christians to have sex before marriage in view of the fact that many are waiting longer to marry?" Another inquired, "Is it permissible for divorced singles to have sex occasionally provided their partners are Christians?" These two questions demonstrate how far we have come down the road of secular humanism's situation ethics. God's moral standards are absolute; the more we tamper with them, the worse matters become.

Any release for sexual pressure outside of marriage is wrong. Under the inspiration of the Holy Spirit, Paul stated, "It is better to marry than to burn" (1 Cor. 7:9, NASB). What could be clearer than that? He did not say it is better to masturbate than burn, nor is it better to be promiscuous—than to burn. Marriage is the only legitimate option to sexual pressure that God has provided. All the vocational, moral, and situational excuses will not change that.

Personally I think God intended people to marry young. A man reaches his strongest sex drive at age twenty-one, and a woman is best equipped physically to bear children from ages eighteen to twenty-five. Only our humanist culture urges us to "wait."

What about the single who must live with sexual pressure because marriage is just not possible at the present? God has promised "a way of escape," but you had better face the fact that in your twenties and early thirties it will be difficult. Throughout life you will have to guard your mind from evil. Particularly avoid pornographic movies, TV shows, and literature. Those images, which can only gradually be erased from your memory, will unnecessarily inflame passions. That's why Paul told young, single Timothy to "flee youthful lusts."

THE SINGLE MENTAL ATTITUDE

Research in recent years has indicated that a person's mental attitude has primary significance. This is particularly true of singles, who face a problem unmatched by their married friends. Couples have one basic mental attitude: "You that are married seek not to be loosed." The singles' mental attitude necessarily is more complex. They must learn genuine contentment in their present state; otherwise they will be miserable. But they also must be open to making new friends of both sexes. In a single's approach to others, an attitude that "I'm not interested in marriage" comes through loud and clear. Remember, your thoughts emit signals to others. This is why an aggressive male or female always on the lookout for a mate seldom finds one. He or she conveys signals of involvement and attachment, driving prospects away before they have ample opportunity to get acquainted.

It is far better for everyone, especially singles, to develop the "others" consciousness to which Paul refers in Philippians 2:3–4. A person who approaches every contact with a sincere desire to learn more about him will never lack for friends. Only a bore will talk endlessly about his plans and activities, then rush off as soon as you mention something you are doing. Such people perpetuate singlehood—and it may be appropriate for self-centered people are hard to live with anyway, unless they learn to be thoughtful of others.

DIVORCEES CREATE ADDED SINGLE PRESSURES

I especially ache for the millions of victims of divorce, particularly those abandoned for "the other woman." I have counseled hundreds of them. These rejected people pursued the same dreams and aspirations for marriage that Beverly and I did. Yet their dreams disintegrated. Now they need help in picking up the pieces of their lives. They know emotional pressure.

My compassion for divorced people extends to other unique pressures that their friends cannot comprehend. Besides rejection, they may well face anger if, like so many, their economic position is worse now than when they were wed. They may also feel the pressure of embarrassment and shame, guilt and remorse. Divorce is a heavy burden for anyone to bear—and even heavier for a Christian. In its rightful exaltation of God's plan of one man for one woman "so long as they both shall live," the church is often intolerant and unforgiving of divorce. Sometimes I think it is easier for some Christians to forgive, love, and accept murderers and prostitutes than the unwilling victims of divorce. And if divorcees should date or talk about remarriage, one would think they had denied the faith and were worse than infidels.

The trauma of divorce and its consequent pressure is sufficient burden for any sincere Christian to endure. Many divorced people are the victims of someone else's lust, selfishness, and sin. Why should they be treated as "untouchables"? These people need our love, acceptance, and companionship, not our judgment, criticism, and condemnation. The thought has often come to me that some Christians will more readily aid physical sufferers than those who hurt emotionally. Our Lord's treatment of the woman caught in the act of adultery (John 8) and the Samaritan woman at the well (John 4) offers a lesson to us all: "Go and sin no more." If He who was absolute holiness chose to forgive the sins of fallen men and women, who are we to do otherwise?

Divorced singles face a major problem in knowing how to handle sexual pressures. How can they make companions of the opposite sex without indulging in moral impurity? If they have learned the art of sexual expression in marriage and established a need for this, they may well be engulfed in sexual pressure shortly after the grief and searing pain of divorce pass. At such a time it is essential that they claim 1 Corinthians 10:13 and ride out the storm of passion; otherwise it will ruin them, both morally and spiritually, just when they really need God's help.

Divorced women have often confided their pet peeve about

dating, so I assume it must be a general problem. Apparently men seldom give the same respect to a divorced date that they extend to an unmarried woman: "You're not a virgin; you've been married." Therefore the divorcee senses that the price of a date includes sexual submission.

A woman needs to understand that giving herself away cheaply may relieve immediate temptation pressures, but creates far more deadly consequences—guilt, embarrassment, and usually a loss of respect that might otherwise lead to the altar. Thirty years of counseling has left me amazed that women fall for the notion that premarital sex will lead to marriage, that is, "If I don't, he will leave me." A good woman doesn't need that kind of man. Single women in particular must understand that a realized need saps motivation; a man will not usually pay the price of getting married if he can get what he wants without it. One of the best motivaters for marriage is unreleased sexual pressure. Not all pressure is bad; pressure can provide extraordinary motivation.

THE PRESSURES OF THE SINGLE PARENT

Probably no group of people in our society experiences more pressure than single parents. Their number has grown rapidly in the past decade. In 1976 there were one million divorces in the United States, the first time that milestone was reached. During 1982, there were 1.2 million, a growth factor of 20 percent in just five years. Sociologists report that the divorce rate is slowing down, but the statistics do not yet reflect this.

As everyone knows, divorce often has longer-lasting consequences for children than for adults. Besides routine life pressures, the children experience loss and heartache, which add to the pressures on their single parents. Because of divorce, at least fifty million children will spend some period of their first eighteen years of life with only one parent. Many of them take out their frustrations on the parent closest to them, compounding the pressures.

A Vocational Necessity

The first major pressure that single parents confront is finding a job outside the home. A national magazine recently indicated that 60 percent of divorced fathers refuse to pay child support. As a result of the women's movement, it is easier than ever for men to walk away from marriage and refuse to bear their responsibilities. Even when a man does pay his child support regularly, it is never enough to take care of that second home.

The options open to a woman in such a plight are usually two: Welfare or work outside the home. Although many women, particularly those with small children, choose welfare temporarily, most women eventually elect to join the work force. Today 56 percent of the adult women work in the marketplace, most of them starting at the bottom because they have few marketable skills.

The divorced male has usually developed a skill and can command a higher income, thus reducing some of his financial pressures. He has another advantage in that he is already used to being the sole support of a family. I well remember when my widowed mother worried continually about possibly losing her job, knowing that we were depending on her biweekly paycheck for our daily food. However, divorced mothers in the work force make very dependable employees. An attorney informed me that he prefers to hire divorced women with children, for a simple reason: They *have* to work.

The single woman may be regularly subjected to sexual harrassment at work. As moral standards continue to decline, the problem will increase. Some men subject hard-working women to great pressures just because they are in a position to do so.

What About the Children?

The pressure that single parents experience *after* a full day of work is sometimes unbelievable. Rushing home to their second "job," they must serve as both mother and father in training, disciplining, and refereeing their children. They have to clean house, do the laundry, iron clothes, fix meals, shop, oversee the budget—and then get organized for the next day. The greatest versatility in the world is developed by single parents who survive.

In my childhood there was a seemingly endless number of

housekeepers. At $5 a week plus room and board, no one kept the job very long. Today there are a few more options, such as day-care centers, preschools, friends, and babysitters, but none of them will replace a loving mother for daytime care.

If you must use a day-care center, find a well-organized Christian school that operates one. Its facilities may not be as lavish as a government-controlled, tax-supported center, but neither will its teaching be secular, humanistic, anti-family, and anti-Christian. The latter kind of teaching creates additional pressures in the home.

Financial Pressure Guaranteed

Simply because of the more demanding lifestyle, single parents almost always face continuing financial pressure. They can hardly go to bed at night without the temptation to worry about unpaid bills. The woman who receives little help from the courts in forcing her husband to pay child support seems to endure an endless chain of financial pressure points. One woman came to us in tears because of these pressures: Her husband had abandoned her with three small children, refused to get a job, and lived on welfare so he wouldn't have to pay child support. She was awarded the home, but had to sell it because she couldn't make the monthly payments. For three years she lived on the equity from the house sale until the Internal Revenue Service required capital gains taxes. Now, with the coffers empty, she was being asked to pay thousands of dollars in back taxes.

For a single parent there is no "Plan B." If he or she gets sick or needs extra income, no one else can come to the rescue. Christians in this situation are confronted by a dilemma when their children are old enough to attend Christian school. If a Christian couple wants to remove their children from humanist-dominated public schools and send them to a Christian school, the wife will probably be forced to seek employment outside the home. This option is not open to the single parent, who must face added financial pressure because of the sacrifice or else feel guilty because he or she is humanly unable to provide a Christian education. At this point the children's grandparents, friends, relatives, or church should remember "orphans and widows in their distress," as the Scripture teaches (e.g., James 1:27).

The pressures described above are only some of those endured by single parents. There are many more. I trust that couples going through divorce soberly recognize that they are very likely exchanging one pressure cooker for a greater one. The gnawing awareness of these pressures added to overwork, lack of time for a reasonable social life, and many other problems leads some single parents to indulge in anger, self-pity, and sometimes another ill-advised marriage. Divorce is rarely the best course of action for feuding spouses who are attempting to resolve marital conflicts.

RETIREMENT HAS PRESSURES

One would think that in the greatest country on earth, retirement would guarantee a time of ease, pleasure, and fulfillment. For some this is true, but even retirement has its unique brand of pressures. In fact, so many people are retiring today that their number is creating severe financial pressure for the social security system. The threat of social security bankruptcy has already stimulated fear pressures in the retired; for many, a solvent system is essential to survival.

Financial security is only one pressure that senior citizens face today. The specters of deteriorating health, loneliness, abandonment, and boredom likewise haunt them. Beyond that, secular humanists are projecting a national program of euthanasia. This is the other side of the abortion issue. If our courts can decree that a human fetus may be murdered through abortion, they can also determine someday that a group of psychiatrists and psychologists can decide when adult life is no longer worth living. The time may come, Francis Schaeffer points out, when America will resemble Hitler's Germany of the middle and late 1930s, when secular humanists controlled society—that is, a senior citizen may not know when the doctor is bringing a health pill or a death pill.[4] This is a pressure no senior citizen needs, and it is one reason why Christians and

---

[4]See LaHaye, *The Battle for the Public Schools*, pp. 203–225.

senior citizens should be at the forefront of the battle to halt the spread of secular humanism.

Fortunately we have not yet progressed that far in the secularization of our society. While the battle is being waged against secular humanism, retirees will have to continue to do what they have always done: Lean on the everlasting arms of a providential, all-loving God who has promised to supply their needs. They should also entrust themselves to the care of their children and family, not the government.

SUMMARY

Pressure is as old as mankind. It follows us like a shadow. It is no respecter of persons. That is why I am challenging you to learn the art of reducing your pressures to livable size before they enslave you. But before we get to the "How," let us survey some pressure spots unique to our day.

CHAPTER 3

Twentieth-Century
Pressure Spots

This is truly an exciting age! We can travel at the speed of sound, astronauts at 24,000 mph, and all take it for granted. Crisscrossing the country on preaching tours, I often muse, "If the apostle Paul had this means of travel available to him, he probably would have seen the entire world turned upside down by the Gospel and not just Western civilization."

Yet travel produces its own brand of pressure. I rush home from meetings to pack, dash to airports, hurry to other meetings, and try to reach three cities in one day. That produces pressure.

Almost all technology generates strain and tension. The twentieth century has been inundated by an "information glut." Who can keep track of everything? Today we become specialists in a few areas and seek experts in others. Pressure mounts as we try to keep abreast of political and societal events. Sometimes pressure is amplified as we fill our minds with global crises and natural disasters on the evening news. No other generation has had the opportunity to view revolutions in South America, civil war in Ireland, a Communist takeover in Asia, and in Africa—all in a half-hour telecast. And that's just international news.

Past generations have endured such upheavals, we know, for historians can identify 251 wars since 1870. But they haven't had to gaze at film clips every night, nor did they always know what atrocities were occurring across town. No wonder their pressures were lesser than ours. In addition, they lived in a society more committed than ours to Judeo-Christian moral values, producing a morally sane society that was safe to live in. The past four decades, which have permitted the uninhibited freedom of expressing "human rights" as established by secular humanist thought, have made our society the violence capital of the world—hardly conducive to an unpressurized way of life. When human suffering and outrage pervade your mind and senses before bedtime, your subconscious mind may continue the mental pressures while your body is at rest, particularly if you are given to fear and anxiety. Instead of awakening refreshed, you are apt to feel pressure as soon as you awaken.

If we add to these the tensions of rapid travel, fast communication, information glut, breakneck schedules, and the tick of the clock, a ready formula for almost insurmountable pressure develops. Since you didn't finish all your work during the day, you take it home, filling the hours when you should be relaxing and enjoying the family. Unless steps are taken to reduce such pressurized living, the individual will eventually experience a breakdown, burnout, or family emotional explosion.

An attorney confided to me that he was contemplating an occupational change. "To stay on the cutting edge of my specialty," he fretted, "if I don't study fifteen hours a week, I can't adequately serve my clients." I asked when he did that reading, and he replied, "At night when I get home or on weekends." Instead of incorporating the extra load into his workweek, he allowed it to spill over into his home life. Of such work habits physical and emotional breakdowns are made, particularly if there is no allowance for physical fitness.

I have always admired construction workers. Physical labor keeps them in shape, and once they have learned the trade, it doesn't take much additional study to keep current. At the end of each day they have accomplished something tangible, satisfied a short-term goal, and finished the day's work activities. Maybe that is why breakdowns seem to be less frequent among construction workers: They endure fewer mental and emotional pressures—as long as there is a building boom. Yet I suspect that every occupation has its pressure-producing side, depending on the individual, his temperament, his mental attitude, and his working conditions. From the beginning of the Industrial Revolution, pressure has been on the increase and undoubtedly will continue to escalate into the twenty-first century. That is the reason for this book. Its purpose is to show us how to govern pressure, no matter what its cause, before it governs us.

THE GROWING FEAR OF A NUCLEAR HOLOCAUST

One nagging fear pervades the hearts of millions of people: The realistic threat of a thermonuclear war that could annihilate civilization, or even a limited nuclear attack that could kill multiplied thousands. Such a possibility is continually paraded before us by the news media and politicians, amid the growing controversy between "nuke" and "no nuke" adversaries.

Ever since President Reagan requested a build-up in U.S. armaments as a deterrent to Soviet attack, our leftist press, educators, and peace advocates of every stripe have been warning us of a potential atomic catastrophe. The possibility that such pronouncements represented a spontaneous outcry was dispelled for me when, during my travels, I viewed the same presentation on four local newscasts. A picture of the city was superimposed over a one-mile area of total destruction and a three-mile area of fallout destruction. Everyone understood the intended message: "Better Red than dead." If you are under thirty, you may not remember the pro-Communist sentiment of the 1960s, but that was the cry: Better to surrender to the Communists than be destroyed by a nuclear war.

This argument creates unbelievable fear pressure in those who are anxiety-prone, as many voters are. This is especially true if they forget the murderous practices of Communist regimes. Red Russians have murdered an estimated 35 million of their own countrymen. In China the Communist "liberators" murdered 67 million. After thirty years of appeasement, disarmament, and unlimited amounts of technological and financial assistance to these international gangsters, little has changed. Some people feel pressure if we rearm; others if we do not. And nuclear pressure is not just limited to governments. I have wondered how long it will be before some terrorist group steals an atomic bomb and attempts to blackmail nations and people into submission.

These gruesome possibilities are enough to distress most people. But when we add to them the international disorders among modern nations during the past four decades and natural disasters such as earthquakes, a person who does not enjoy a vital relationship to the living God may well succumb to the intensified pressures of our world.

Christians should *never* let themselves get pressured by world events.

First, our Lord said, "When you see wars and rumors of wars, see that you are not troubled" (Matt. 24:6). And He added, "Do not let your hearts be troubled. Trust in God; trust also in me. In my Father's house are many rooms; if it were not so, I would have told you. I am going there to prepare a place for you. And if I go and prepare a place for you, I will come back and take you to be with me that you also may be where I am. You know the way to the place where I am going" (John 14:1–4, NIV). In other words, don't allow temporal events to unnerve you: "Trust in me; I have an eternal home in heaven waiting for you." A minister remarked to me: "If an atomic bomb ever fell on me, it would simply blow me to heaven." That kind of faith neutralizes the nagging fears of international disaster.

Second, this world will never be destroyed by an atomic or nuclear holocaust. I know this because our Lord predicted that when He returns for His church, people will be "marrying and giving in marriage." In fact, they will even be "eating and drinking" merrily, perpetuating routine existence until His coming. "Just as it was in the days of Noah, so also will it be in the days of the Son of Man. People were eating, drinking, marrying and being given in marriage up to the day Noah entered the ark. Then the flood came and destroyed them all. It was the same in the days of Lot. People were eating and drinking, buying, selling, planting and building. But the day Lot left Sodom, fire and sulfur rained down from heaven and destroyed them all. It will be just like this on the day the Son of Man is revealed" (Luke 17:26–30, NIV). The Book of Revelation describes various activities that will take place on earth during the days of tribulation that will yet "try [pressure] the whole earth" (see Rev. 3:10).

I am not saying that Russia will not attempt to black mail our leaders into subjection with the threat of thermonuclear war. This is why we need to elect godly men and women of moral commitment to every governmental position in our nation. I *am* saying that in these unsettled times we do not have to experience the pressure caused by fear which those without God must face. To them it is a realistic source of continual pressure; they neither have a refuge from fear nor believe or know of the prophecies God has given concerning the future.

THE PRESSURE OF VOCATIONAL INADEQUACY

Another significant pressure plaguing many of the 99 million men and women in the work force today is the growing threat that advancing technology may automate them out of a job. Just a few years ago a person could learn a profession or trade and expect to practice it throughout life. We have mentioned the trend toward specialization today. If that specialized endeavor becomes obsolete, the specialist must be retrained.

The twelve thousand air traffic controllers who were fired by the U.S. government serve as an example of $35,000-to-$50,000-a-year specialists suddenly put out of work—with no comparable skills to offer in the marketplace. Admittedly they were not automated out of their job, but they do illustrate how quickly specialists can become an endangered species. Factory workers are particularly beset by these problems. As steel and auto companies mechanize their processing plants and assembly lines to stay competitive with foreign imports, many workers have watched their occupations diminish or disappear.

Can you imagine the pressure produced by the word *unemployable?* It represents a pressure cooker to every conscientious worker. Also facing this threat today are coal miners, garment workers, farmers, schoolteachers, and even lawyers— because there are so many of them.

INFLATION, RECESSION, AND DEPRESSION

The fear that runaway inflation would create a deep recession generates widespread mental pressure. Conservative economists predict that someday we will have to pay for our one-trillion-dollar national debt through a national or world-wide depression. An economist-friend points out that the U.S. is actually $2 trillion in debt because the treasury already owes another trillion in guaranteed retirement benefits to government employees, armed services personnel, and social security payments.

Who knows whether these possible disasters will befall us during our lifetime? We cannot give full credence to either the prophets of doom or the economic optimists. The free enterprise system has proved itself amazingly resilient, but nothing is guaranteed. That is why the Bible teaches, "Put not your trust in princes, nor in the son of man, in whom there is no help" (Ps. 146:3). In other words, never place your confidence in stocks or bonds—or even your government. Rely only on the Lord! If we have to face depression (as many Christians already have done), our Good Shepherd will guide us, care for us, and supply our needs then, just as He always has.

However, faith is no substitute for planning and hard work. God's teaching throughout Scripture challenges the child of God to a "faith that works" lifestyle. The psalmist knew he could trust God to save him from Goliath, but he also understood that he had to pick up his sling, select five smooth stones, and advance upon the enemy. I have never seen God overrule that winning combination: Man does his part and God does the rest.

For that reason, a wise person evaluates his skills in light of the marketplace. Usually your job will not be eliminated by automation overnight. You will more than likely have ample opportunity to seek the Lord's direction in upgrading your skills. One is well-advised to do so periodically anyway. An expansion of skills leads to occasional advancement and lays the foundation for vocational change, which not only eases the pressures of job insecurity, but also alleviates the additional pressures of vocational boredom.

One tool that may aid you in selecting the best vocation is a temperament test that I have prepared after fifteen years of study on human temperaments. It will diagnose your primary and secondary temperaments and offer you fifty vocational possibilities for your temperament companion. Many have used it in preparation for vocational realignment; women unfamiliar with the job market have found it helpful in discovering the best field to pursue for a life vocation. For information, you may write to Family Life Seminars, P.O. Box 1299, El Cajon, California 92020.

A business executive in our church had an interesting experience. As the assistant chief in a large plant, he had the oversight of four supervisors, and one of them was openly campaigning for his job. The chief and the young supervisor were both heavy drinkers; the latter went into debt for a swimming pool and used it to "wine and dine the boss." To make matters worse, the chief considered my friend a "weak leader," because he didn't curse and drink with the supervisors. When I asked him how he intended to respond, my friend answered, "I will do what I have always done: Put in the best days of work that I can, and trust God." During the next six months the pressure became intense at times, and frequently he asked for prayer. Then one night he came to prayer meeting with a big smile. "Guess what happened today? My boss was transferred and was replaced by an old friend I worked for fifteen years ago." Asked about the ambitious supervisor, he replied, "He is stuck with me and six more years of payments on his swimming pool!"

Someone may ask, "What about office politics?" This can be a problem and in some cases become a pressure point even for a Christian. Through the years I have watched godly men and women illustrate Romans 8:28 many times. All things *really do* work together for good for God's children. Being certain of this before trouble starts is an emotionally healthful factor that prepares us when the testing period strikes.

WHAT ABOUT WELFARE?

An examination of vocational pressure would not be complete without at least a brief look at welfare. "Is it right for Christians to be on welfare?" I have often been asked. "Why not, as long as they don't abuse it or become enslaved by it?" I respond.

Welfare was never intended by God or its initiators as an

embarrassment to the truly needy or as a lifetime means of support. It originated as an emergency system to help people in time of need. Unfortunately it has been abused into the billions of dollars and to the demotivation of millions of lives. Today we can identify second- and third-generation welfare recipients.

If you ever find it necessary to avail yourself of the welfare program, do it with self-respect. Many relatives, friends, and Christian brothers have paid into the program to make it possible for widows, minors, the unemployed, the disabled, and others to be supported through difficult times. Look at it as a temporary assistance program that will enable you to upgrade skills or seek other employment as soon as possible. Thank God for it. A rule of thumb: Use it, but don't come to rely on it.

THE PRESSURES OF THE HANDICAPPED

Possibly the most pressurized life situation is that of the physically handicapped person. Since World War II our nation has increasingly regarded these people as an untapped resource. During the war many were given specialized training and placed into jobs never before open to them. Today they appropriately receive special consideration. A free and compassionate society like ours can well afford to relieve much of their pressure, enabling them to live as full a life as possible.

I have found that one of the most important needs of many handicapped people is to accept their lives, despite all the limitations, as a gift from God. This is the first step toward learning how to effectively live with these limitations. It is unrealistic for the disabled to try to compete with the nondisabled on equal terms; it is better for them to discover what they can do best and excel at it.

Joni Eareckson Tada has had a vital testimony both in and out of the church. Unable to use her hands or legs, she draws by holding an art pencil in her teeth, speaks eloquently, and sings. Once when we saw her, she excitedly shared the news, "I'm getting married!" God has led her step by step from one agonizing plateau of faith to another, just as He guides us. But it all started when she accepted her limitations and looked to God to use her life.

Admittedly life is not easy for disabled people; but when

they find that special niche God has for them and learn to live within their limitations, their pressures are greatly reduced.

A handicapped man is the film editor of our television program. According to our director, "He is the best I've ever worked with; in fact, he has lightning hands." His legs are crippled, but his heart, mind, and hands qualify him to run a million-dollar computerized editing machine that rents for $300 an hour. He is married and lives as close to a normal life as possible. Millions of such courageous people have learned to trust God to live above their circumstances rather than beneath them. They are an inspiration to us all.

LIVING WITH A HANDICAPPED CHILD

Ever since Adam's rebellion and mankind's fall, sin has brought disease and sickness into the human race. In most cases it arises, not from the sin of the parents, but from mankind's sin in general. Jesus healed a certain blind man. Asked by His disciples, "Who sinned, this man or his parents?" Jesus replied, "Neither this man nor his parents sinned, but this happened so that the work of God might be displayed in his life" (John 9:3, NIV).

Those special children who are physically or mentally handicapped have come into many homes. Parents of such children are provided by God with a special love for them because they truly need it. As a pastor I have seen some beautiful examples of Christian and parental compassion bestowed on the retarded, crippled, blind, or others born with physical limitations.

Until our oldest daughter bore our fifth grandchild, I had always viewed handicapped children from a distance. Jeremy was born with a serious hearing disability. One ear lacks a canal and is totally without hearing; the other ear functions at a level of only 50 percent. Like many handicapped children, Jeremy has developed various compensating traits; for example, he is extremely bright and very lovable. Perhaps his loving nature is a reflection of the love that has been showered upon him by his parents and brother and sister since birth. At age five, he is not yet aware that he is "different."

Such an "angel unawares," as Dale Evans so beautifully

called this kind of child, brings pressure both to parents and to siblings. The greater the handicap, the greater the pressure, of course. But God has promised to give grace according to our need. Parents who are raising normal children may not possess the grace necessary to raise a handicapped child. But to every parent with such a child, our heavenly Father has promised compensating grace in abundant supply. Consider these assurances: "My grace is sufficient for you" (2 Cor. 12:9), and "My God shall supply all your needs according to his riches in glory by Christ Jesus" (Phil. 4:19, NASB).

Remember God's principle: The greater the handicap, the greater the grace.

Last year a family of six lost the Downs Syndrome son they had raised for fourteen years. At birth the doctors predicted the child's expected lifespan to be from six months to four years, but through tender, loving care he enjoyed fourteen birthdays. After his funeral the family reminisced about the contribution he had made to their lives. No one mentioned the extra care, the added burden, and the pressures he had brought into the lifestyle of a normal, active family. Instead each member recited how his life was enriched by having had this lad in their home for fourteen years. All agreed they were a closer, more tightly knit, and loving family because God had given him to them. This reminds me of our Lord's words, "Give, and it shall be given unto you" (Luke 6:38).

THE PRESSURE OF THE EMPTY NEST

"Many couples fail to prepare themselves for their children's graduation from the home," warns Henry Brandt, a Christian psychologist and a close friend. When I heard him make that statement many years ago, I didn't understand what he meant, for all our children were still living at home. Today I understand. The children have graduated from school and established their own homes; we have reverted to our original marriage status: All alone. In truth, we love it!

Raising children is a wonderful experience that I recommend to everyone. But sooner or later children leave the "nest"; that is God's plan, so you should prepare for its happening. If your life is invested solely in raising your children, you will not be prepared when graduation comes. Many couples experience depressing silence and emotional void at that time. A tragic phenomenon, even in the church, is the increasing number of veteran couples in this situation who get a divorce. This condition is accelerated by two factors.

First, the partners are not "best friends." Marriage is for companionship, but they have not used the first twenty to twenty-five years to build a deep friendship. When the children leave, the most unifying factor in their relationship has vanished. Many such marriages fall apart, usually to the surprise of their friends.

Second, the wife has developed insufficient outside interests. Consequently she almost seems to be starting her life over. At such a time many women go into a deep depression; others seek employment; some get involved in immoral relationships. This kind of situation can be averted if proper priorities are maintained between your role as (1) partner, (2) parent, (3) person. As important as parenting is, you should not make it your entire life. When children are young, they demand most of your time; as long as they live in your home, they should have high priority. But they must not consume your entire life.

The older your children become and the fewer you have living at home, the more you should involve yourself in the life of your partner and the lives of others. Whether in a vocational field, Christian service, or volunteer work, everyone needs to do something for someone. The loss of your children will occasion some pressure, but if you do not have meaningful activities planned to fill the void, the pressure will be greatly intensified.

In spite of all my activities as a busy pastor and writer, I felt one of the saddest days of my life when our daughter Linda left us, traveling 2,500 miles to a Christian college. Our family of six was never quite the same again. But that is as God would have it. Our children are on loan from God for eighteen years or so; after that they are to build their own families. It's all part of the cycle of life, but it certainly isn't the end of the world. God has other things in store for those who would serve Him.

My wife Bev exemplifies this truth. Without realizing it, she gradually prepared for our children's graduation. When they were little, she spent 90 percent of her time as a wife and mother and 10 percent as a junior department Sunday school superintendent. As the children grew older, she developed other interests. To supplement our income, she did typing in the home. Then the two oldest started to attend a Christian high school. With more discretionary time available, she spent one day a week putting out the church paper; she later added the church bulletin to her schedule. After the two oldest were in college, she served as the registrar of Christian Heritage College for five years. After two children married and a third entered a Christian college, she began speaking at banquets and women's conferences and eventually wrote three widely accepted books. After our youngest went away to college, she joined me as a speaker at Family Life Seminars around the country. Since then she has founded and become president of Concerned Women for America, one of the largest women's organizations in the United States. Now we co-host a weekly television program, "LaHayes on Family Life," and she continues to write books.

Looking back, I realize that her present round of activities was fashioned very gradually. Had she not been willing to take the first little steps of faith fifteen years ago, she would not now be taking giant steps. Along the way, she has been a mother, confidante, and companion to her children, whose departure was a source of joy, not emptiness. And although she has many close friends in our church and her ministry, her very best friends are Linda, Lori, Lee, Larry, Murph, Sharon, and Greg —her children and their mates—and me, of course.

THE PRESSURE OF A BAD MARRIAGE

There is nothing in life better than a good marriage and few things worse than a bad one. Our Creator instituted marriage to be a fulfilling, productive, and rewarding experience. When it isn't, there is something drastically wrong, and usually the error starts with one or both partners' relationship to God. In counseling others I have found that a person's affinity for his mate is a good indication of his relationship to God. You cannot maintain a holy relationship with God and be estranged from your partner. Harboring anger, bitterness, or resentment toward one's companion will destroy communion with God. That is why marriage problems should be approached from a spiritual perspective.

I have spent much of my life in marriage counseling and training people at seminars, on radio, and now on television for a happier family life. Thus dealing with thousands of people, I appreciate the pressure a bad marriage creates. Personality conflicts, sexual dysfunction, widely different interests, mixed marriage (believer with nonbeliever), spouse abuse, and just plain selfishness—all create pressures that cannot be released by handball, exercise, or even divorce. In fact, division usually produces more pressure, not less.

If you are facing such pressures, whether great or small, it is crucial to seek help. Don't be too proud to consult your pastor or a Christian counselor. The church offers the greatest support in these matters today. Christian counseling supplies biblical solutions to human problems on every conceivable subject in family relationships. The church provides its members and community with marriage and family training films, study sessions, family-life seminars, couples retreats, Bible instruction, and regular worship services and Sunday school. This is one reason why church marriages, though not always perfect, are generally far happier and less pressurized than any others in today's society.

Like a toothache, a bad marriage will not heal itself. You need assistance in relieving the pressure before it gets worse. Your church is the best place to obtain that help.

THE PRESSURE OF ALIENATION OF AFFECTION

Everyone needs love! That is the main reason people get married: To give and receive love. When that love dies or is pointed in an illegitimate direction or toward an illegitimate object, heavy and hurtful pressure ensues. This pain is reaching epidemic proportions today. It is the principle cause of infidelity, sexual sin, and divorce.

In no other age has there been more sexual temptation than in our own. Sexual permissiveness as presented on television is undermining moral values in the home and, moreover, is advocated as normal and common. Pornographic literature, both "hard" and "soft," inflames carnal passions. Add to this the fact that the average married person spends more time at work in close relationship with members of the opposite sex than he does consciously with his mate at home—a potentially volatile emotional and sexual mixture. I have seen an alarming increase in adultery and division caused by infidelity during the past ten years, even among professing Christians. Until you have sat for hours with these hurting people, you have no idea what pressure infidelity can cause.

However, alienation does not always include immorality. Through strength of character and moral, spiritual commitment, a mate may "fall in love" with another person but be true to his partner. Although such faithfulness is commendable, it still puts pressure on the home and the people in it. Fortunately, unfulfilled desire usually is short-lived, and the feeling passes.

Such feelings are symptomatic of a deeper problem: Wrong thoughts. Love is perpetuated by positive thoughts about someone, but is assassinated by negative thoughts. If you want to slay your love for a person, simply harbor negative or critical thoughts about him or her. Even the strongest love may be snuffed out in ten days to three weeks by this means. Yet you can ignite love by the reverse process. If you reject negative thoughts and think positively about your partner (Phil. 4:8) for three weeks, your love will return. To many whose love has died, I have advocated this process: Make a list of ten qualities you like about your partner; thank God twice a day for those traits and do not permit negative or critical thoughts to dwell in your mind. Within three weeks, I promise, your love will return.

THE PRESSURE OF A LOST LOVE

The other side of the coin is your reaction when you are faced with pressure from the loss of your partner's love.

A single person may find that the burden of unrequited love does not last a lifetime; gradually his love will fade, and his life will return to normal. Not so the married person, committed for life, when his emotional radar detects that a partner's affection is shared with another.

Studies show that almost all couples fear the possibility of unfaithfulness. One man whom I know has kept his wife in a state of anxiety for twelve years. Since no adultery is involved—or at least is verified—she does not consider divorce an option, and she is forced to live with her torment daily. However, I have watched her grow spiritually while her husband, by comparison, has deteriorated. She seems to be the happier of the two, whereas he is a "double-minded man, . . . unstable in all his ways" (James 1:8). Everything he touches sours. He seems to place more pressure on himself than on her.

When your love is not returned or you sense something is wrong with the relationship, take an inventory as to the cause. Have you been critical, nagging, or resistive lately? Do you dash your mate's plans and aspirations? You may have inadvertently contributed to the problem. I have counseled some couples and had no trouble understanding why one partner did not love the other in the face of constant criticism and disapproval. Such treatment opens the door and makes a partner vulnerable to that "other person."

This pressure tends to arise in the late twenties or early thirties, when the male sex drive is strongest and the wife's body is too weary for romance due to bearing two or three children in quick succession. In addition, his vocational pursuits are likely to take his body and mind out of the home for long periods of time.

The best preventive measure against such pressures is to examine with the Bible the basic needs of each partner and work toward fulfilling them. According to Ephesians 5, a man needs honor and respect as a leader; a woman needs love. I have yet to counsel a couple when the wife has honored the husband and he has loved her. Such partners have no need of counseling. This doesn't mean that successful couples never have difficulty; rather, it means they can usually resolve problems on their own.

In addition, no person can love someone other than his mate and be controlled by the Holy Spirit. According to Galatians 5:22, the first characteristic of the Spirit's control in one's life is "love." You can always be sure that the love that emanates from God will *always* be pointed in the right direction.

PLAN FOR MARRIED COUPLES

During my years of counseling others I have developed a special plan to keep love fresh and alive for all married couples. No matter what their age or stage of life or marriage, all couples should have *quarterly mini-honeymoons.* Save your money, put it in your budget, but whatever it takes, schedule a weekend (or Friday night and Saturday) mini-honeymoon four times a year.

This gives the wife confined to the house with small children something to look forward to, it provides the busy husband a goal to work toward, and it offers the couple a special time to cultivate their love. This need not be an expensive venture: Dinner for two, a drive to another city, a special night in an affordable motel, and a time of relaxed fun. The price, whatever it is, will prove to be a sterling investment in a happier marriage.

THE PRESSURE OF AN AILING MATE

Few people anticipate having to face physical handicaps in the early years of marriage. When they do arrive, they produce pressure for the entire family proportionate to the severity and kind of disability. I have watched partners walk with their mates through the dark valleys of everything from polio and strokes to paralysis and blindness. Without exception I have found that adversity brings out the true character of a person. Henry Brandt has said at our seminars, "Pressure doesn't make your spirit, it reveals it." That is, what you are under pressure is what you really are.

The army used to declare, "When the going gets tough, the tough get going." As we shall see in chapter 7 each temperament responds differently to pressure; but sickness, accidents, and real disability usually bring out the best in people. For Christians that best should be His strength made perfect in our weakness, His grace revealed in our time of need.

Your wedding vows read, "I take you to be my wedded spouse . . . for better or for worse, in sickness and in health till death do us part." The minister proclaimed you husband and wife "so long as you both shall live." Every married couple seals their pledge with this sacred vow. Marriage is a commitment for life—for the newlyweds struck by a truck as they happily speed through the streets of Minneapolis pursued by their well-meaning friends, leaving the bride paralyzed from the waist down, and for the all-American football star made paraplegic by polio. This fact helps you to live with the pressure, but it does not relieve it.

Our family learned something of the pressure occasioned by illness in the early seventies when a dune buggy accident in the desert inflicted Beverly with a severe case of rheumatoid arthritis. It could not have come at a worse time for me: Two of our children were still living at home, and I was pastoring a growing church, serving as president of Christian Heritage College, holding thirty Family Life Seminars a year, and writing the book *How to Win Over Depression*.

Every day that Bev's health diminished, my pressures increased. Diagnosed by Scripps Research Clinic as incurable, she was told to prepare herself to spend her life in a wheelchair. Barring a miracle, her case was said to be irreversible.

We tried everything. Starting with prayer, we went the full course from eating watermelon rinds and lotus leaves to visiting chiropractors and arthritis specialists. We even examined an acupuncture series and a powerful-smelling ointment in Tijuana. (I found that when those we love or when we ourselves are hurting, we will do anything and pay any price seeking help.) For three years, every night I was home I operated a chiropractic vibrator or a rented ultrasound machine to reduce her swelling. Every morning we immersed Bev's hands in a wax bath solution ten times and then wrapped them in towels for twenty minutes just to help her start the day. The twenty-one aspirin tablets prescribed at Scripps created intense ringing in her ears and affected her personality.

Whenever we heard of a new treatment, we would look into it. Bev's travels took us to Santa Barbara, California, where a doctor prescribed a specially prepared vitamin N formula strong in niacinamide (the best relief she has yet discovered).[1] In Houston she went to a doctor who prescribed high doses of thyroid and fergon with vitamin C. Several years ago we spent

---

[1]R-A-Formula, 2411 Calle Linares, Santa Barbara, California 93109

two weeks in a clinic in Bucharest, Romania, where she was introduced to GH3. Many times I would hold her hands in mine, and we would pray in faith, believing that God would perform a miracle and heal her. Today she is 90 percent better. Whether it is the power of prayer or the medication which she still takes regularly, or a combination of both, we don't really know. We do believe God guided us through unique circumstances to Bev's current improved status, which essentially holds the disease in remission except when she gets overtired.

I tell all of this for two reasons: (1) to show you that pressure caused by illness is no respecter of persons; and (2) to inform you that we ourselves have experienced some illness-related pressures. We have personally learned that "God's grace *is* sufficient" for our need. One side effect from all this pressure has been to draw us closer to God than ever before, and it has truly enriched our love for each other. I have seen this happen to many couples who have been forced to endure illness.

THE GRIEF AND SORROW OF DEATH

Thomas Holmes of the University of Washington studied the causes and results of stress on humans for twenty-five years. His findings are regarded as classic in the field. We will examine his entire scale in another chapter, but here I will introduce his most significant discovery: The greatest pressure-producing event in all of life—earning 100 points on Dr. Holmes's scale—is the death of a spouse. You can understand why he ranks this so high: The more you love someone, the more seriously you feel his death. Since death is inevitable, it is a specter that plagues those who love deeply; this specter causes increasing degrees of pressure throughout life.

There is no way to avoid this kind of pressure except by preceding your loved one in death. Non-Christians have little hope in this life and none in the life to come, so their pressure is great. When an atheist commits his loved one to the ground, it is like burying a dead animal: It's all over. What a tragedy! A person who believes in God (as most people do), but one who has no personal faith in Christ is almost equally pathetic. When he walks away from his loved one's grave, he "hopes" to see him again or "believes" he may, but lacks assurance.

Not so the Christian. We sorrow at the loss of loved ones, of course, but our sorrow is different. We are confident that we will see our loved ones again. According to Paul, our faith in the second coming of Christ and our ultimate resurrection, guaranteed by God Himself, means that we "sorrow not, even as others which have no hope" (1 Thess. 4:13, KJV). Consequently we come away from the experience of death "with hope," confident that our loved one will one day rise again. Our belief in the resurrection does not eliminate the pressure of grief, but it reduces it and shortens the period of sorrow.

THE PRESSURE OF CARING FOR AN AGED PARENT

Whenever two families share a house, pressure is inevitable. Temperament and the duration of such a situation will affect the amount of pressure. The need to care for an aging parent is a common pressure, and you should plan for it.

Usually aged parents must come to live in the home of their married children. Ideally this occurs after the grandchildren have graduated into their own households, but that isn't always the way life works. Many times a family is forced to make the choice of abandoning the grandparents or tackling the project of making room for them joyfully.

During the past fifty years, a peculiar national attitude has developed: "It's government's responsibility to care for the elderly." Advancements in medical science, vocational safety, and other factors have lengthened life expectancy in the United States (by more than fourteen years since 1929), and the cost of housing has led to smaller homes. It is no longer a case of reopening a bedroom in the old farmhouse and planting a few more rows of vegetables. Moving grandma and grandpa into your home can create pressure for everyone.

Regardless of circumstances, grandparents are our responsibility. We are commanded to honor our parents (Eph. 6:1–3). He does them no honor who remands his parents to some senior citizen's center unless it truly is better for *them*. Sometimes, of course, it is. Bev's mother and blind stepfather shared our home for three years at a time when our children were still living at home. After he died, Bev's mother lived alone until an illness made this impossible, at which time she went to live with Bev's sister. Bev's mother married again at age eighty-three, and she and her husband moved into an ideal Christian Community in Sebring, Florida. But such facilities are rare.

Welcoming Bev's stepfather into our home when he became blind created pressure on the entire family, but God supplied our needs, and the experience proved to be a blessing. One benefit was that our children learned respect for their senior relatives: Just because they are old, we don't abandon them. Part of our Christian testimony is fulfilling our responsibilities in caring for our family both old and young.

Like every other pressure in life, this must be managed—either removed or else reduced to manageable size. When you invite relatives into your home, let them know that they are welcome guests, but that the home is yours: You are the head, you raise the children, you make the decisions. They must cooperate by living within established guidelines. Some may think this is not being loving and respectful, but quite the opposite is true. If you fail to delineate their rights and responsibilities, any difficulty they may cause in the family is your fault. Even when there are deliberate hindrances on their part, loving confrontation is the best method of dealing with knotty problems. One can disagree with a parent without dishonoring him.

Remember, your children will learn how to treat you someday by the example you set for them.

SUMMARY

This book cannot deal with all the pressure-producing circumstances of life. But these two chapters describe the major stages of life and the basic situations that cause the greatest pressures. If your specific situation has not been dealt with, examine the causes and results of your unique pressure. As we investigate the management of pressure, you will be able to define a method of your own for handling it.

It is important to remember that everyone encounters pressure. Life itself is pressure. Because the removal of all pressure would destroy you, you must learn how to manage it. To do this, you must first examine what causes it.

CHAPTER 4

The Causes of Pressure

Pressure is like a hot-air balloon. Sometimes the balloon is filled to capacity; at other times there is so little air inside that the balloon can barely stay aloft. Naturally we prefer the latter situation in terms of pressure. At such times we are not really aware of pressure, for we are enjoying moments of ease and relaxation. We focus upon pressure only when it has reached gigantic proportions, influencing our every thought and feeling.

Before we can manage giant pressure and reduce it to size, we must examine its major causes. The next page displays a formula that captures the essential ingredients of pressure.

Life is pressure. We have learned from the two previous chapters that whether one is a newborn offspring, just leaving the dark warmth of mother's womb and suddenly confronting the bright, sterile, and sometimes cold delivery room of life; or a senior citizen, awaiting the doctor with his last medication; or somewhere in-between, life begets pressure. According to one realist, "the only place where we can avoid pressure is the cemetery."

Students of stress have found that the events of life often generate bearable if not welcome pressure. As a father, do you remember the birth of your first child? As your wife was experiencing enormous physical pressure, yours was mostly emotional, but it was real—and good. Pleasurable events do not

The CAUSES of PRESSURE

EVENTS of LIFE

+ CHANGE

+ PEOPLE

+ LOSS of CONTROL

+ NO HOPE in SIGHT

= PRESSURE

usually create adverse pressure, but adverse circumstances certainly do, and it is easier to cope with the former than with the latter. The pressure of that childbirth brought a combination of exhilaration and weariness, which is not difficult to manage provided it is not protracted. You may recall that the pressure existed in direct proportion to the time in labor.

Joyful events create pressure that usually will not bother us, because it is short-lived. My hobbies of snow- and water-skiing both create a certain kind of pressure for me. I am forced to work out months in advance to be in shape for such activity, jogging consistently to keep my wind and legs in condition. And then I confront the pressure of packing, traveling, shopping, unpacking, standing in line at the ski lift, and so on just to experience those few mad moments of exhilaration and freedom. Sometimes, when I go too fast, an unusual amount of pressure builds. And what do I gain from all this activity? Stiff muscles, mountains of bruises, and a damaged ego. Yet I proudly announce, "Wasn't that terrific?"

Joyful pressures are brief and healthful. But so are many work pressures. Meeting deadlines, keeping appointments, finishing projects—these can elicit great positive pressures if we maintain the right attitude toward work.

Thus work is never an enemy; only drudgery becomes onerous. Two people can perform the same task side by side, and to one it is enjoyable, to the other a bore. Why? What if you were the bored one?

First, you may be a round person in a square hole. That is, you are doing something you were never meant to do or trying to be something you shouldn't be. We will perceive this more clearly when we treat the subject of temperament. If your job demands meticulous care and perfectionism, but you are not detail-conscious by nature, you have the wrong job. By contrast, if you are pursuing a selling job, but are an introvert by nature, don't be surprised if every confrontation with people triggers inordinate pressure. Usually pressure is reduced to livable proportions as we repeat a function until we feel "comfortable" doing it. If the pressure intensifies long after your training period, you probably need a new line of work. The task for which you were designed will give you pleasure.

Second, your work may be drudgery as the result of your mental attitude. Many working women, for instance, are getting bored with the marketplace. Millions of working mothers would rather be homemakers, tending to the children at home rather than serving in some office or restaurant. This mental attitude, producing great pressure, will not subside. You should seriously evaluate your circumstances to see if the second income is really necessary. If not, quit. Some working women find that by the time they pay higher taxes, child care, transportation, and other expenses, they increase their family's take-home pay by only 12 to 30 percent. If you have to keep working, however, in order to provide your children with a Christian education or to augment your family's income, change your thinking process to one of thanksgiving. The fastest way to intensify life's pressures is to gripe or develop an ungrateful spirit. Obey the biblical command, "In every thing give thanks: for this is the will of God in Christ Jesus concerning you" (1 Thess. 5:18, KJV).

I have found myself musing, "If I were someone else, living somewhere else and facing difficult circumstances, I would still confront pressure and problems; and they would be worse, for I would be out of the will of God." Paul's words offer great comfort in this regard: "I have learned to be content whatever the circumstances" (Phil. 4:11, NIV). If Paul could say that from a cold, damp Roman prison cell, certainly we can assume the same mental attitude *whatever* our life's circumstances.

CHANGE

Change is a natural part of life, yet it almost always produces pressure. The more unexpected the change, the more intense the build-up of pressure. Some changes are obviously more significant than others. For example, a traffic ticket creates pressure, but it can hardly compare with the death of a close relative. If enough serious pressure-producing changes occur within a certain period of time, the stress can ruin or impair your health. Many have experienced nervous breakdowns in just this kind of situation.

The classic research on this subject was made by Thomas Holmes and Richard Rahe of the University of Washington

School of Medicine. For more than twenty-five years they analyzed the effects of change on five thousand patients, studying the results of stress on these people in an attempt to predict the probability of illness arising from various degrees of change.

In my book *How to Win Over Depression*, I reprinted, by permission, the Holmes-Rahe scale, which has been widely used as a self-awareness tool. I had noticed in my research that the same changes they listed were often followed by depression. The process is change followed by self-pity, which—if it persists long enough—will always produce depression. Frequently the severity of the self-pity is directly proportionate to the significance of the unexpected change. In other words, it isn't solely the change that creates our depression, but our mental attitude toward the change.

Dr. Holmes's research is still relied on heavily by writers on business motivation management, medicine, counseling, and stress. To my knowledge, it has not yet been equaled. For this reason I am equating the entire list of forty-three life-changing events with the most common causes of pressure. A medical writer, Keith W. Sehnert, wisely modified this scale in his book *Stress/Unstress* to bring it up to date with current lifestyles.[1] Because of inflation, Dr. Sehnert raised the mortgage limit from $10,000 to $40,000 in items 20 and 37. In addition, he dropped the last three categories—"Vacations; Christmas; Minor violations of the law"—and replaced them with 41, "Single person living alone"; 42 and 43, both "Other—describe." Some life-changing events that trouble people were not listed, such as "Bankruptcy" and "Rape"; Dr. Sehnert did not assign a specific amount to these problems, but rather asked each reader to assign a personal estimate of how much pressure that event produced. The entire scale is reproduced here so that you can score yourself.

---

[1] *Stress/Unstress* (Minneapolis: Augsburg, 1981), 68–69.

HOLMES-RAHE SCALE
Revised by Sehnert

Instructions: Mark the events that have occurred within the last twelve months. Circle or fill in its value. Enter the total at bottom.

Event	Value
1. Death of spouse	100
2. Divorce	73
3. Marital separation	65
4. Jail term	63
5. Death of close family member	63
6. Personal injury or illness	53
7. Marriage	50
8. Fired at work	47
9. Marital reconciliation	45
10. Retirement	45
11. Change in health of family member	44
12. Pregnancy	40
13. Sex difficulties	39
14. Gain of new family member	39
15. Business readjustment	39
16. Change in financial state	38
17. Death of a close friend	37
18. Change to a different line of work	36
19. Change in the number of arguments with spouse	35
20. Mortgage over $40,000	31
21. Foreclosure of mortgage or loan	30
22. Change in responsibilities at work	29
23. Son or daughter leaving home	29
24. Trouble with in-laws	29
25. Outstanding personal achievement	28
26. Spouse begins or stops work	26
27. Begin or end school	26
28. Change in living conditions	25
29. Revision of personal habits	24
30. Trouble with the boss	23
31. Change in work hours or conditions	20
32. Change in residence	20
33. Change in schools	20
34. Change in recreation	19
35. Change in church activities	19
36. Change in social activities	18
37. Mortgage or loan of less than $40,000	17
38. Change in number of family get-togethers	15
39. Change in sleeping habits	15
40. Change in eating habits	15
41. Single person living alone	—
42. Other—describe	—
43. Other—describe	—
Total	—

If your total score is 200 or less, it is not likely that your present accumulated life changes will cause an emotional or physical breakdown, provided you have not developed a negative thinking pattern that unduly protracts the normal pressures of life. If your score is 300 or more, you may have a 50-50 chance of physical or emotional difficulty during the next two years. Dr. Sehnert suggests that "you are well-advised to take it easy for a year or so with any major decisions. Not making a decision to change is an acceptable option."[2]

Whatever your score, you should study chapter 6.

APPLYING THE SCALE

After reading *How to Win Over Depression*, a woman called me one night from a distant state. Her husband had just been committed to a psychiatric hospital. Having read the Holmes-Rahe scale in the book, she calculated that he had totaled 512 points in a one-year period, including divorce, remarriage, change of job, a new business with a big mortgage, a new home, and collapse of the business. Humanly speaking, his mental breakdown is not surprising. Only a mature, Spirit-controlled individual with a very positive mental attitude could handle all that change and accompanying pressures.

Dr. Sehnert offers a case study of a neighbor who investigated a job opportunity in another state. After discovering that he had already accumulated 300 points on the scale, he decided that more change would threaten his equanimity, so he turned down the offer. That was probably a wise decision, yet many times life makes these choices for us. I am convinced that most people who endure severe pressure in life could avoid some of it if they plan ahead instead of letting life just happen.

PEOPLE

One inescapable cause of pressure in life is people. Some people can be relaxing, loving, and invigorating; we find others irritating and exasperating. Some develop pleasant, winsome associations; others are so cantankerous that they can't get along even with themselves.

---

[2]Ibid., 69–70.

"Personality conflicts" form the most common cause of disharmony between individuals, from the home to the marketplace. In some instances we can remove ourselves from people, but this is not always possible. Ultimately all of us are likely to be forced into a social or work situation with an "impossible person" who can instantly create pressure for us. And running away is not always an option.

"I can't stomach him!" we commonly exclaim. The pressure generated by an individual when we are around him sets off so many stress hormones in our system that we may get "ulcers." Other people can induce high blood pressure and even heart attacks. This is particularly true for a person who is very hostile by nature; his inner animosity usually spills over and disrupts his interpersonal relationships with all others.

Hostility tends to aggravate every adverse tendency a person possesses. When he has a "bad day," it is usually because one person sets him off early in the day, and this intensifies all adverse traits—from ego, selfishness, and greed to abrasiveness, lack of consideration, and meanness. Such individuals increase not only their own pressures but everyone else's.

A significant misconception, however, is that other individuals make our "spirit." Actually they merely reveal it. True "peace, love, and joy" will not be destroyed by other people, because it comes from God, not man. Anyone can react in anger to a hostile person, but what seems "natural" is likewise "sinful." Consequently, if we "walk in the Spirit," other people will not trigger pressure within us.

Practically, I have found it very helpful to try to analyze why people act as they do. This is one of the benefits of knowing the four basic temperaments, which will be discussed in chapter 7. If I know a person's temperament, I can almost preduct his reaction in a given situation. Thus his response becomes less threatening to me as an individual; consequently I am less inclined to oppose him and more equipped to accept him.

Nowhere is this more useful than in a marriage relationship. Since opposite temperaments usually attract each other in marriage, an aggressive extrovert often selects a hesitant, deliberative introvert as a partner. Consequently, reaching a decision or even discussing options can be a pressure-producing experience. Temperament differences can generate enormous pressures in any interpersonal relationship. But when you understand that certain actions or reactions are a reflection of the other person's temperament, the pressure of relationships can be diffused more easily.

LOSS OF CONTROL

Looking back on recent months of personal pressure, I find that it became acute because for a time I had lost control. Anytime we do not govern a situation, pressure will mount.

Have you ever received, as I once did, a statement from the Internal Revenue Service alleging that you owe them $600 when you thought your taxes were paid in full? I had purposely not taken all my deductions so as to avoid receiving such a notice. In my case, my accountant verified after much research that the IRS was wrong; I didn't owe additional tax. As soon as control was established, the pressure eased—at least until I received the accountant's bill for his services.

A number of years ago, my schedule required that I drive through metropolitan Los Angeles every Monday morning and evening in order to study. The venture was always exhausting! I found that as soon as I entered the Los Angeles city limits, my blood pressure rose 10 percent or more and my nerves became taut. The reason? In contrast to San Diego's system, Los Angeles freeways are out of control. Drivers dart in and out, cut you off, stop quickly, honk their horns, tailgate other vehicles—it's crazy! It seemed that all seven million residents of the Basin area were swarming onto the freeway at the same time.

By contrast, when I came within fifty miles of San Diego on the return trip, I relaxed, my blood pressure returned to normal, and I enjoyed the drive. What made the difference? I was back in control. I am used to a 55 percent freeway glut, not Los Angeles' daylong 125-percent traffic. I simply am not conditioned to handle that kind of driving pressure, yet millions of people in metropolitan areas drive to and from work every day under those same conditions. No wonder there are so many emotional breakdowns, heart attacks, ulcers; so much hypertension and even alcoholism. Whenever we lose control, pressure soars.

Stationed in Germany as a G.I. after World War II, I worked my way up to administrative clerk for the chief of staff and deputy chief of the 9th Tactical Air Command. The chief was a full colonel, the deputy chief a lieutenant colonel. Since my office was situated between theirs, their visitors had to approach my desk. The lieutenant colonel loved to put pressure on other people—privates, sergeants, majors, and especially second lieutenants. His deep, stentorial voice resounded through my office. But when he entered the colonel's office, his voice rose in pitch, and he became tense and nervous. Why? He maintained full control in his own office, but in the "old man's" office he exercised no control.

The colonel was the ranking officer in our building, so he was usually very relaxed and in control. But there was the time when three-star General Joe Cannon paid a surprise visit to our headquarters: The colonel's pressure meter soared!

Pressure increases or decreases, therefore, in direct proportion to the degree of control we are able to exercise over circumstances, finances, relationships, vocation, and our every endeavor. This is probably why disorganized people who never plan ahead or rarely do things the same way twice seldom succeed in life, seeming to stagger from one life crisis to another.

Jere E. Yates is chairman of the Business Administration Division at Pepperdine University. He cites the research of two different studies that identify the effects of control or loss of control on groups of people in relation to their ability to tolerate irritating noise levels.

One group worked under noisy conditions but was given the option of pressing a button if the noise became too irritating; the other group did not have this option. Most of the people in the first group completed their work without pushing the button. When their work output was compared with that of the second group, it was found that those who worked in the noisy environment without the button made errors on reading tasks and arithmetic problems, showed little tolerance of frustration, and were unwilling to do favors for other people. People in the other group who worked under equally adverse conditions, but who *did* have the option of pressing the button, showed almost none of these after-effects. The reason for the difference in productivity is quite clear: People in the latter group believed they could press the button and stop the noise if they chose to do so, and as long as they believed they had this option (even though the button would not actually work), the results would be the same. . . . Your perception of reality is the basis for your behavior even though reality may be somewhat different from your perception of it.[3]

It is evident from this study that a person's perception of how much control he exercises over a given experience determines how much pressure it causes in him. Suppose two young fathers, each with three sick preschoolers at home, are preparing to go to work. One kisses his wife good-by. The other says, "Honey, if it gets too rough, just call me at the office and I'll come home and help out. When I get home tonight, I'll take over the care of the children and give you a break." Which wife will experience the greatest pressure during the day? Probably the one who was kissed. Ironically, the second husband may have to work late and will not get home until the children have gone to bed, but the fact that his wife could have called him if necessary gave her the element of control she needed to ease her daytime pressures. Observe your own activities during the next few weeks and watch how being in control reduces pressure to livable levels, whereas being out of control intensifies them.

> The importance of the feeling of being in control was also confirmed by researchers in Stockholm, Sweden, who studied the stressful effect of going to work by train. The researchers found that even though passengers who got on the train at the beginning of the line traveled for an hour and 40 minutes, they experienced considerably less stress than passengers who got on midway and traveled for only 50 minutes. The researchers used the "feeling in control" concept to explain this curious phenomenon: Passengers who boarded the train early had far more control over where they sat, with whom they sat, and how and where they arranged their personal belongings than those who boarded the train when it was almost full. Thus, you may be able to tolerate greater amounts of physical stress if you also feel that you are more in control.[4]

---

[3]Jere E. Yates, *Managing Stress* (New York: AMACOM, 1979), 41.
[4]Ibid.

Keith W. Sehnert, who studied this Swedish research project, made this observation:

The Swedish Train Study

Scientists in Sweden were able to measure the amount of a stress-related hormone, epinephrine, in the urine of volunteers who took the commuter train to Stockholm. Group One got on the train at the first stop, 79 minutes away from the city, while Group Two got on the train midway, 43 minutes away from their destination. Although both groups agreed that the ride got increasingly stressful as they approached Stockholm, those commuters who got on the train *first* actually secreted *less* epinephrine. Those who boarded the train first felt a greater freedom of choice. They could choose their preferred seat, find plenty of room for coats and briefcases, and even sit with their friends. The key factor was *control*. Those who boarded midway had to scramble for seats, sit with strangers, and adapt themselves to situations in which they had little control. The result for them was a more stressful ride in to work each day, and they gave chemical proof of it in their urine samples.[5]

A California freeway study that corroborates my own freeway experience was also noted by Dr. Sehnert.

The California Study

Scientists at a California university attached pulse monitors to the wrists of executives who were instructed to keep a diary of their activities each day. The diary was then correlated with the record of their pulse rates. When the data were analyzed, the scientists found that the highest pulse rates were found in the volunteers who drove on the freeways. The process of dodging cars, fighting traffic jams, and watching for unexpected stop lights presented situations with one thing in common: These drivers felt they *lacked control*.[6]

THE IMPORTANCE OF CONTROL

The National Institute for Occupational Safety and Health (NIOSH) did an in-depth study of working conditions to determine the degree of stress on employees. Their findings were quite surprising. Most people would guess that the most stress-driven workers are a workaholic businessman, a neurosurgeon, or an airline pilot. Yet none of these was in the

---

[5]Sehnert, *Stress/Unstress*, 41.

[6]Ibid.

thirty jobs cited at *the top of the list.* Rather, this is what the scale of the most pressurized vocations looked like, according to the study:

1. Health technicians	16. Photographers
2. Waiters, waitresses	17. Telephone operators
3. Licensed practical nurses	18. Hairdressers
4. Quality-control inspectors	19. Painters, sculptors
5. Musicians	20. Health aides
6. Public relations staff	21. Taxi drivers
7. Laboratory technicians	22. Chemists
8. Dishwashers	23. Bank tellers
9. Warehouse workers	24. Social workers
10. Nurses' aides	25. Roofers, slaters
11. Laborers	26. Secretaries
12. Dental assistants	27. Registered nurses
13. Teachers' aides	28. Machinists
14. Research workers	29. Bakers
15. Computer programmers	30. Metal workers[7]

Examining this scale carefully, you will make an interesting discovery: The higher up a profession is listed on this pressure scale, the less control an individual has over himself, his job, and his working conditions, but the more exposure he has to *people.*

I was amazed at first to find health technicians, waiters, and waitresses at the very top. What do they have in common? People, people, and more people. Subsequently I interviewed many waiters and waitresses, asking why their job is so stressful. (Some 99½ percent of those in the serving business are willing to express their opinions on this subject, and this confirms the study's findings.) In every case their answers boil down to *lack of control.* Consider the following:

"Our cook never prepares the food the way I order it."
"Our soup is never hot."
"The busboys take no pride in their work."
"No one seems to care."
"Some customers are real stinkers!"
"Most people are nice, but some people are impossible to please."

---

[7]Ibid., 38–39.

"I really don't like this kind of work, but I'm not trained for anything else."

These sample responses all reflect the frustration that builds when a person has to work under circumstances over which he has no control. Such pressure is graphically accelerated if the person feels trapped and sees no end in sight to the problem.

AIR TRAFFIC CONTROLLERS

I was surprised to find that the NIOHS study of the most pressure-filled jobs did *not* rank air traffic controllers among the top thirty. It may be that they were not included in the study because there are only twelve thousand in the entire country compared with more than one million waiters and waitresses.

When President Ronald Reagan fired air traffic controllers for refusing to live up to their signed contract, the entire nation became aware of them and their pressurized vocation. A study of the history of the controllers at O'Hare Airport in Chicago, one of the busiest in the world, verified the incredible tensions of this occupation.

The O'Hare Air Traffic Control Study

This study involved a review of the medical records of the 94 controllers and trainees at Chicago's O'Hare Airport. It showed that only two had worked there for more than 10 years. The records also showed that two-thirds of the employees had ulcers or symptoms of ulcers, more than 35 controllers had been removed for psychiatric reasons since 1970, and the incidence of high blood pressure was four times as frequent as that found in pilots checked by Federal Flight Administration medical examiners. The reason for such findings was the feeling by these employees that they not only had to make split-second decisions that affected the lives of hundreds of passengers, but they often felt they were *not in control* because of many factors such as weather, pilot error, and equipment failures.[8]

Heavy traffic areas are not the only cause of pressure. One foggy day I landed at the John Wayne Airport in Orange County while I was out of practice with my instrument-flying technique. I don't mind instrument landings at San Diego, for I have the

---

[8]Ibid., 41–42.

approach patterns memorized; but I had never before landed at John Wayne on instruments. My first approach was ragged, so I declared a "missed approach," went back up to 3,000 feet, and flew over the VOR (ground station). The air controller was very patient and understanding even though he was busy with other traffic in the area, for he knew right where I was and could confirm that I was following the prescribed pattern for a missed approach.

On my second approach I came in a quarter of a mile south of the runway and broke through the clouds at 1,100 feet. When I saw where I was, I radioed the controller to "cancel my IFR [instrument flight rules] flight plan"—I would go in visually. I did not realize that in my nervousness I had not pushed the radio button deeply enough, so my message was not transmitted. Consequently when I banked my plane to the left to start a 270-degree turn that would put me in line to make my final approach turn, that pleasant, friendly controller screamed at me! In a tight, demanding voice he announced, "Twin Cessna niner hotel hotel [9HH] climb immediately to three thousand feet on a heading of three-three-zero [degrees]."

I was too nervous to return to the fog, so I replied, "Negative! I called you and canceled IFR."

He screamed again, "Negative! Did not receive! Proceed as instructed! Other aircraft in the area!"

I got the message, and although I could see the runway by this time, I obeyed his orders and successfully landed on my third attempt. To his credit, he offered a mild apology as I lined up the third time; and this helped to reduce my pressure—a little.

I am sure my procedure did not help that controller's ulcer! He was not disconcerted by the fog, the traffic, or even a rusty pilot who had to go around again. Only the loss of control rattled his composure. When he lost control of my whereabouts, his decision could have jeopardized every other plane for which he was responsible.

"Control" is one sphere in which Christians have a special advantage in life. It is not always possible to govern life circumstances. For example, students cannot dominate teachers (though they sometimes try), but are subject to tests or assignments. A Christian can reduce normal pressure as he passes through a time when everything seems "out of control," because he can literally obey the precept, "Commit your way unto the Lord, *trust* also in Him," knowing that "He will direct your path" (see Ps. 37:5; Prov. 3:6). Life is never out of control when God is in control. You may not know exactly what He is doing with your life at the moment, but it is comforting to know that His providence will prevail. This verse has been helpful to me: "And let the peace of God rule in your hearts, to which also you were called in one body; and be thankful" (Col. 3:15, NKJB). "Let the peace of God rule" suggests that we trust His direction rather than our plans, resources, or circumstances.

NO HOPE IN SIGHT

A chief cause of pressure build-up, creating harmful stress, is the absence of hope. If you encounter several adverse situations, recoil from a host of difficult people, suffer through unexpected change, and feel out of control, you *must* be able to see light at the end of the tunnel. If you can't, you are in trouble. Without hope of eventual relief, whatever pressure you feel at present will be intensified. If that situation persists, it can be dangerous.

A human being cannot live without hope. According to Hal Lindsey, "Man can live about 40 days without food, about 3 days without water, about 8 minutes without air, but only 1 second without hope."[9] I'm sure Hal was exaggerating slightly for effect, but his point is well taken. Proverbs 29:18 declares, "Without a vision the people perish." Without a goal, hope, or dream, any person begins to die.

Last fall I experienced the greatest pressure period of my life, and lack of hope intensified the pressure in my soul and spirit. I had made the most significant change of my life, resigning the pastorate of a great church with a growing, multifaceted ministry after twenty-five years. Somehow I knew that I had just terminated my thirty-two-year career as a pastor of local congregations. I was excited about the change and never

---

[9]Hal Lindsey, *Hope for the Terminal Generation* (Old Tappan, N.J.: Fleming H. Revell, 1976).

doubted that it was the will of God, yet it was an enormous step of faith. With a stable church having an annual budget of over $1.6 million, a school budget of $4 million, a college budget of $2 million, and other ministries, I was responsible for a $10 million program. At that point I turned it all over to someone else and started at about ground zero.

The lack of a strong financial base was not my primary concern—I had lived by faith before. But the enormous cost of television production boggled my mind. More than $275,000 was required for set and thirty-nine weeks of production costs the first year. Another $700,000 was necessary for purchasing of air time and for film reproduction, and $150,000 would be expended as we held 125 banquets all over the country. Can you imagine what it's like to eat chicken (the least expensive banquet menu) 125 times when you really find chicken distasteful? Even the threat of dying from chicken poisoning can cause pressure.

During those early months, as I watched the money pour out and the income trickle in, my pressures mounted. Looking back, I can diagnose the cause of those sleepless nights and numbing pains in my head, back, stomach, and side: Loss of control with no end in sight. For a time my staff and I had lost control of our expenditures, and there was no possibility of raising the money needed to stay on television. After we agonized in prayer, God led us to shift to a more experienced group of consultants, who brought control into the organization.

Then two miracles occurred. A large gift came from a person deeply interested in our ministry, and this paid for thirteen weeks of production costs; and I signed a contract with the publishers of this book, which had a royalty arrangement that provided certain funds for the television ministry. As we toured the country, sharing our burden for America and her hurting families, a growing number of people responded to our challenge and took a step of faith with us, becoming monthly faith partners in making our vision of a family life program (which does not ask for money on TV) available to every city in the United States. Slowly our average monthly deficit shrank from $40,000 to about $12,000.

That didn't solve our problems, however, because we knew

it would take at least another year just to break even. But it did introduce a measure of control to the management of our organization and presented a glimmer of light at the end of the tunnel, which made all the difference in the world to my spirit. Finally the intense pressures generated by our unique step of faith eased. I also began to utilize many of the principles of the Spirit-controlled life that I have written about in my other books, and I can testify that they really do work!

WHAT ABOUT YOU?

Are you experiencing pressure these days? If so, ask yourself these two important questions:

1. Have I lost control?

2. Has the light gone out at the end of the tunnel?

If your answer is yes to either of these, give serious thought to making whatever changes are necessary to bring control back into your life and its experiences. Then look to God for the faith He alone can give. He promised, "I will never leave you nor forsake you, . . . and lo, I am with you *always*" (see Deut. 31:5; Matt. 28:20). Hope never flickers when God's presence permeates your situation, but you can negate all the future blessings He has prepared for you by losing sight of this truth.

Victory in Christ does not exempt you from pressures that the trials and activities of life produce, but He will see you through them all. Remember, He promised to preserve you, not from experiencing pressure, but from being destroyed by it.

THE GREAT COMPOUNDER

One final cause of pressure—one that always compounds whatever other pressures you face—is guilt. People suffer from guilty consciences because they are human beings and not animals. Contrary to secular humanist teaching, we did not evolve from a lower form of life. This is important, because one of the unique characteristics God has created in mortals is conscience. Humanistic psychologists can never adequately help people until they realistically face this fact of human nature.

Another uniquely human characteristic is free will. Those who obey the laws of God (which are written on the table of their conscience) do so voluntarily. He did not fashion us as robots, programmed to obey Him automatically. Consider the examples of Adam and Eve, Noah, David, Moses, and scores of other Bible characters. Those who obey God do so as an act of will. But disobedience is also a choice. And it is related to the problem of guilt.

Champagne and wine are offered free on many air flights. I am so Scotch by nature that it is difficult for me to refuse anything that is free. But Scripture teaches that a Christian should not "be drunk with wine wherein is excess" and that pastors and deacons should not imbibe strong drink. (Note that the wine of Bible days was at least 50 percent weaker than that available today.) But who is to know? At 37,000 feet I could drink and no one would know the difference—except that my conscience constrains me.

The same can be said for pornography, lustful thoughts, dishonesty, cheating on one's income tax, and marital infidelity: Your conscience always knows. Unless you have "seared your conscience" by extensive abuse or have educated it into submission through the skeptical "wisdom-of-man" training offered in secular education today, it will intensify all your pressures whenever violated. You ignore it at your peril.

WHAT IS GUILT?

Guilt is the mental, emotional, and spiritual pressure that results when a person violates his conscience and the laws of God. It produces shame and remorse, destroying one's self-acceptance and confidence toward both God and man. It is usually accompanied by a feeling of dread or apprehension regarding the penalty that must be repaid by one's deeds, either in this life or in the life to come. This pressure, left unattended, can rob a person of peace, love, and joy, compounding all other problems and pressures.

People do not experience guilt identically. The warm, bubbly person of sanguine temperament is capable of pushing to the back of his mental file cabinet his deceit, making light of his "mistakes," which he rarely calls "sins." Eventually these actions and their consequences build inner pressures until the sanguine collapses in repentance.

The hard-driving choleric has by nature the most underdeveloped conscience. This born leader is usually painfully honest, but is inclined to violate his conscience if he can rationalize somehow that the end justifies the means. He usually tries to still his conscious mind by working diligently or giving something to the person he has cheated, offended, or injured. Rarely will he apologize.

The easygoing phlegmatic is usually careful not to violate his conscience. He tends to act circumspectly. When guilt does build up, he finds it difficult to repent because he does not show emotion easily and can be really quite stubborn. When he does repent, however, he experiences great relief.

The temperament with the most sensitive conscience is the melancholy. He may feel guilty even when there is nothing to feel guilty about. Conscientious and perfectionist by nature, he usually experiences tremendous guilt feelings if led to violate his standards and the commands of God. Additionally, he may indulge in self-condemnation even after he gains the forgiveness of God and the offended party.

People experience guilt differently, but all feel it. Guilt produces pressure. In fact, guilt pressure can break some people who do not experience any other heavy pressures. You can imagine what it does to anyone who is already being traumatized by pressure. No wonder so many people resort to alcohol, hard drugs, or medication to gain relief; they don't really solve the problems or reduce the pressures, but they do ease the pain. However, when the person sobers up, the pressure returns—and often greater than before.

HOW TO COPE WITH GUILT

There is only one way to handle guilt properly: Face it head-on. Ignoring it will not help; you must seek God's only remedy, the cleansing blood of Jesus Christ, His Son. That is why He came to this earth in the first place: "To cleanse us from all unrighteousness" (1 John 1:19, NASB). But His cleansing is not automatic. The Bible makes it clear that forgiveness is granted only after one confesses his sins to God in the name of Christ. God takes care of the rest, for Scripture teaches that our sins are washed away. Even more important, "He remembers them against us *no more*" (see Jer. 31:34; Heb. 8:12).

Some people just cannot dismiss their sins. Conscientious souls have trouble forgetting their sins even after God has forgiven and forgotten them, and this continues to add to their pressure. Even though their guilt is unrealistic, it does the same damage as true guilt. This is where faith has significance. If we take God at His word, we will recognize that sins confessed in His Son's name are truly forgiven. If you have confessed your sins, they are indeed forgiven—even though you may remember them.

For this kind of guilt pressure, proper therapy comprises three practical steps.

1. Do a Bible study on God's forgiveness and the cleansing of sins. Write down all the verses on these subjects you can find; synthesize them on one or two sheets of paper. In doing this, you develop your own commentary on the subject based on God's Word.

2. Every time confessed sin comes to mind, verbally thank God by faith for His forgiveness.

3. Do not permit your mind to dwell on the subject. One of my counselees was so guilt-ridden that she could gain relief only by actually putting her finger on the verse—1 John 1:9—as she gave thanks for God's past cleansing. Gradually God's peace overcame her unnecessary guilt pressure.

I have found that Christians who honestly face and confess their sins with a true sense of repentance are usually blessed with the sweet peace of cleansing. Without this they will find little joy in their life. This is the reason why carnal and unrepentant Christians are so miserable.

When I encounter a repentant Christian who does not experience this peace, I find that one of two problems is present: (1) He does not understand the nature of God. His concept of God is not of a merciful, loving, heavenly Father. Therefore he needs to do a Bible study on the person and nature of God; (2) He fails to love and accept himself as the Bible teaches. These two misconceptions will increase guilt, and guilt will compound pressure. Fortunately there is a remedy for both problems.

CHAPTER 5

The Good News
About Pressure

Although pressure is inevitable, there is good news: Pressure isn't always bad. Indeed, if we learn the art of handling pressure, we can do more than manage it; we can use it to our advantage. Later in this book I will show you how to use pressure to accomplish more work. But first we must consider the relationship between pressure and stress.

During the past two decades scientists have discussed stress extensively, and authors have penned many helpful books on the subject. My library includes no less than fifteen of them. Yet none agree on the nature of stress, probably because they have failed to distinguish between pressure and stress. Most combine the two, but I am convinced that pressure comes first, producing a degree of stress on the body.

Consider these definitions of the important qualities of pressure, stress, and distress:

Pressure: The emotional and mental reaction to the ever-changing activities of life.

Stress: The physiological response of the body to pressure. The greater the pressure, the greater the stress. Not all stress is harmful, for without it there is no motivation, achievement, or even preservation of life itself. Depending on the nature of the pressure and a person's mental attitude, stress can be either positive or negative.

Distress: The harmful results of negative stress that the body is not able to absorb or adapt to. When protracted, it can cause sickness and even premature death.

Certain kinds of life events faced with a positive mental attitude can produce beneficial pressure . . . which in turn activates positive stress . . . which ignites certain glands and hormones . . . which in turn can impart energy, alertness, drive, and a feeling of exhilaration or joy.

By contrast, the events of life *faced negatively* will produce negative pressure, which results in negative stress called distress. The human body was amazingly designed by our Creator to compensate for the negative effects of pressure, *if* it is not indulged for too long. Distress is nothing more than negative pressure experienced over such a long period of time that the human body is unable to cope with it. The end of this protracted negative pressure and stress will ultimately be illness, mental breakdown, suicide, physical crippling, or death. The following diagram illustrates basic truths of life.

No one lives a static life. Some very passive individuals may appear never to experience pressure, but inwardly they really do. You do not live that way. How do I know? You are reading this book. Passive people usually do not read books unless forced to and then they often fall asleep in the process. This is particularly true if they see a suggestion coming that would solicit a change in their passive lifestyle.

More than 95 percent of the population experiences the rising and falling tides of life and the sensations of pressure, stress, and distress.

STRESS AND SELF-PRESERVATION

One of the first philosophical principles I learned in school is "Self-preservation is the first law of life." Many people confirm that when they are faced with a challenge, crisis, or a stress-producing event (called a stressor), something mysterious takes place that supplies new reserves and power they lacked previously.

During my junior and senior years of college, I also ministered in the Oolenoy Baptist Church of Pumpkin Town, in the

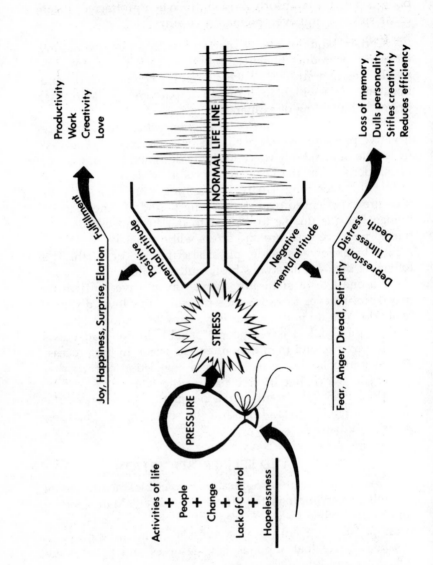

foothills of the Blue Ridge Mountains of South Carolina. About two-thirty one morning, a young man was driving his expectant wife to the hospital. The clay dirt road was so slippery that the front of his Model A Ford ended up in a ditch. Talk about pressure—he was petrified! With superhuman strength he slid the front of the car back onto the road with his bare hands. The next day—after the safe arrival of the baby—he tried to demonstrate his great strength to his friends. To his amazement, he could not budge his car. Why not? Stress was not energizing him.

THE SELYE RESEARCH

The most prominent researcher in the field of stress and its effects on the human body was Hans Selye, the Austrian-born endocrinologist. For more than thirty years he dedicated himself to research in this field. The following personal interview with Dr. Selye was reported by Walter McQuade and Ann Aikman in their book *Stress:*

"Experience counts. I am at least ten times more effective than I was at twenty-five. But I have lost so much because of deterioration."

An intimation of Selye's life work came to him in his early manhood. He recalls, "I was a second-year medical student in Prague when my professor brought in five patients for the students to diagnose—one with cancer, one with gastric ulcer, et cetera. It struck me that the professor never spoke about what was common to them all, only about the differences. All these patients had lost weight, lost energy, and lost their appetites. Had I already been a physician at that time, I wouldn't have thought about it, but as it was, I asked my professor if I could work on it in my free time, but he thought it was silly.

"That was in 1926. Ten years later, as assistant professor at McGill in Montreal, I was trying to isolate a hormone in the laboratory. I was working with extracts of cow ovaries and injecting them into rats. All of the rats, when later subjected to stress, had the same reaction—adrenal overreaction, duodenal and gastric ulcers, and shrinking thymus, spleen and lymph nodes. The worse the stress the stronger the reaction. Then I tried injecting other materials, even simple dirt. I even tried electric shock, and got the same results."

He also tried inducing fear and rage in the laboratory animals. Again he got the same physical results. From this puzzling beginning, in which he discovered the existence of a generalized reaction to almost any kind of stress, he gradually groped toward the conviction that the endocrine glands, particularly the adrenals, were the body's prime reactors to stress. He says, "They are the only organs that do not shrink under stress; they thrive and enlarge. If you remove them, and subject an animal to stress, it can't live. But if you remove them and then inject extract of cattle adrenals, stress resistance will vary in direct proportion to the amount of the injection, and can even be put back to normal."

Selye defines stress as the nonspecific response of the body to any demand made on it. He explains that when the brain signals the attack of a stressor—which could equally be a predatory beast, or a threatening office memorandum—the pituitary and adrenal glands produce such hormones as ACTH, cortisone and cortisol, which stimulate protective bodily reactions. If the stress is a fresh wound, the blood rushes inflamatory substances in to seal it off; if the stress is a broken bone, swelling occurs around the break. The pro-inflammatory hormones are balanced by anti-inflammatory hormones, which prevent the body from reacting so strongly that the reaction causes more harm than the injury.[1]

The human body's ability to adapt to many life-threatening situations has long intrigued me. Blindness in one eye, for example, intensifies the sight of the good eye. The loss of hearing in one ear often brings improvement of hearing in the other. Medical personnel are able to acquire immunity to infectious diseases that surround them. The same is true, according to Dr. Selye, of stress and pressure: They can actually increase a person's capability, energy and productivity. He describes the process this way:

As we have now begun to run into technical terms, let me explain a few: The adrenals are endocrine glands situated just above each kidney. They consist of two parts, the outer layer (or cortex) and the inner core (or medulla). The cortex produces hormones that I called corticoids (such as cortisone), whereas the medulla secretes adrenalin and related hormones, all of which play important roles in the response to stress. The thymus (a large lymphatic organ in the chest) and the lymph nodes (such as can be felt in the groins and armpits) form a single system usually referred to as the thymicolymphatic apparatus, which is mainly involved in immune defense reactions.

---

[1]Walter McQuade and Ann Aikman, *Stress* (New York: Bantam, 1974), 16–17.

It soon became evident from animal experiments that the same set of organ changes caused by the glandular extracts were also produced by cold, heat, infection, trauma, hemorrhage, nervous irritation, and many other stimuli. Here was an experimental replica of the "syndrome of just being sick," a model that lent itself to quantitative appraisal; for example, now the effects of the most diverse agents could be compared in terms of the adrenal enlargement or thymus atrophy that they produced. This reaction was first described, in 1936, as a "syndrome produced by various nocuous agents" and subsequently became known as the general adaptation syndrome (G.A.S.), or the biological stress syndrome. It has three stages—(1) the alarm reaction; (2) the stage of resistance; and (3) the stage of exhaustion. . . .

Because of its great practical importance, it should be pointed out that the triphasic nature of the G.A.S gave us the first indication that the body's adaptability, or adaptation energy, is finite. Animal experiments have shown that exposure to cold, muscular effort, hemorrhage, and other stressors can be withstood just so long. After the initial alarm reaction, the body becomes adapted and begins to resist, the length of the resistance period depending upon the body's innate adaptability and the intensity of the stressor. Yet, eventually, exhaustion ensues.[2]

Dr. Selye's three stages of stress are basic to the problem, and they should be examined carefully.

1. The Alarm Stage

When the pressures of life, be it threat to one's person or purse, are experienced by the body, a message goes to the pituitary gland in the brain where the hormone ACTH (acrenocorticotrophic hormone) is made. This ACTH travels through the blood stream and activates the adrenal glands and other hormones. They in turn cause the body to experience many other changes, such as palpitation of the heart, increased blood pressure and breathing rate, release of sugars and fats into the system, and tension of the muscles, which provides the fuel and oxygen for quick action and strenuous energy.[3]

The parishioner who was rushing his wife to the hospital had no idea all this was taking place in his body, but the resultant superstrength proved it was. However, this pressure-pro-

[2]Hans Selye, *Stress Without Distress* (New York: New American Library, 1974), 25–26.

[3]Sehnert, *Stress/Unstress*, 20

ducing stress does not just aid physical activity. The same reaction to stress will help the accident victim or the operation patient to clot his blood, ease his system through shock, and intensify his hearing and other capabilities, thus enhancing his chances for survival. This self-protective stage is usually of short duration.

2. The Resistance Stage

After the immediate threat disappears, the body relaxes and returns to normal base line. The pulse, blood pressure, and breathing rate slow down and return to normal levels. The pupils that were enlarged to improve the range of vision become smaller. The tensed muscles of the legs and arms, ready to fight a foe or run away to a safer place, relax. The digestive system, that had ceased functioning so that extra blood could flow to the muscles and brain, resumes its normal movement and digestive functions. The bladder and kidneys, that had dramatically slowed down, now can speed up and return to their normal function—often bringing the strong urge to urinate.

3. The Exhaustion Stage

If the actual or perceived danger continues over a prolonged period of time, a new stage begins that can end in disease or, in certain cases, death by exhaustion. Protracted wear-and-tear can affect any of the body's organs or systems. In the case of the arteries in the cardiovascular system, there may be such continuous spasm that a condition develops called hypertension (high blood pressure). The increased blood-clotting mechanism may create a clot in a small vessel in the heart leading to a myocardial infarction (heart attack). Other types of wear-and-tear problems will depend on the physical and hereditary makeup of the individual. Examples include peptic or duodenal ulcers, heart rhythm abnormalities, diabetes, and nervous colon.[4]

It would seem that the first and second stages can often generate positive reactions. When they have run their course, they cause little or no damage to a person. The human body has an amazing flushing system that can expel this excess hormone. Usually after a good night's sleep, the individual has no further ill effects. The third stage is quite different, breaking down the body through protracted response to stress. We will investigate this process in the next chapter.

---

[4]Ibid., 21.

Naturally varying degrees of stress exist in each of these stages, depending on what life events trigger the pressurization that sends the stress hormones into action. In moderation these can be beneficial. I have long noticed that some employees need this kind of pressure to be energized to work. A newspaper office is a good example. Compare the tempo of work at 8:00 A.M. with the pace at thirty minutes before the printing deadline.

It is a wise person whose forward-planning procedures can keep some degree of pressure on him at all times. Goal-oriented people appear to be more energetic than others. I am not convinced that this is true; it's just that their goals and plans keep a good degree of pressure on them, which makes them more active. This tends to prevent them from experiencing the very high and the resultant low emotions felt by others.

Mental attitude is the key. A bad mental attitude always increases negative pressure (or distress), whereas a good mental attitude—though not always able to eliminate pressure and stress—does reduce it so as to become positive. A good mental attitude can turn distress into positive stress. That is why I keep repeating, "Your mental attitude, not your circumstances, determines the degree of your pressure." A positive mental attitude is the key to learning to cope with pressure.

I have been a sports nut most of my life. To keep sports in balance, because of time limitations I only permit myself to get vitally interested in professional football. For three years I directed the San Diego Chargers' weekly Bible study, and I discovered that athletes thrive on pressure too. With some players, it is the World Series or football playoffs: They seem to call upon superstrength reserves that are absent during the regular season. Some players who become complacent on one ballclub get a new lease on life after a trade to another club. So it is with many people. I am convinced that many people who retire early really need a change of job, location or, in all probability, mental attitude more than retirement.

Always remember: Pressure is inescapable. Instead of trying to flee from it, learn how to use it. Naturally you will have to discover your pressure tolerances, for each person has his own level. Find yours and stay within those limits. But don't try to avoid pressure; refuse to look on it as an enemy. Within certain limits, pressure-producing stress can be your friend; it all depends on your mental attitude.

CHANGE ISN'T THE REAL CULPRIT

I would like to take exception to many professional counselors. I am inclined to believe that the principal ingredient in producing pressure is not change, but one's mental attitude toward change. The pressure generated by change activates helpful ACTH hormones that increase our energy and improve our capability to cope with the change. In addition, change itself comes many times for our good. For instance, I can remember how upset our children became when confronted with the need to change schools. Around our home there was literally "weeping and wailing and gnashing of teeth," but relatively soon the groans faded and the new school turned out to be better than the old one.

Whenever a top-level manager is transferred from one department to another, the change creates pressure for those working under the new manager. Some employees have even been moved to tears. Yet in a few weeks everyone is back to normal, the pressure has vanished, and people are happily doing their work. Obviously all that emotionalized response to pressure was superfluous. The pressure seemed acute at the time, but in essence it was unnecessary. It was not caused by the change, but by the way a person perceived the change.

So it is with life. Most of the changes that generate pressure are real, but they frequently produce unexpected benefits physically, personally, or vocationally—unless our mental attitude is so negative that change can never be anything but a source of pressure. We can understand when an unsaved person allows his pressures to overcome him, but that should never be the case for the Christian. The latter can resort to Romans 8:28, discovering that all things do indeed "work together for good." Some Christians instinctively discard the good, because they will not accept change as being from God.

Even people-induced pressure can be "good" if we don't negate the power of God working in our behalf. Admittedly, some people can be exasperating. Students of human temperament often ask me, "Which temperament is the most difficult to get along with?" I always reply, "The selfish temperament." Those who have no consideration for the rights and feelings of others not only alienate others, but become a strong cause of pressure. These people, of course, seriously need our help.

A computer representative in our church told me about a man whom he "just couldn't stand." He was both a cause of pressure for my friend and a threat to his spiritual life. At my suggestion my friend began to pray daily for this man—for his family, business, and personal problems. Soon my friend acknowledged, "I can't really understand it, but I am beginning to love this man. My pressure is almost gone, and I no longer dread it when he comes around." Months later my friend led him to Christ; today he works for his former antagonist. We often forget that God can change people; yet He can also change our attitude toward them.

Give mental assent to the good news about pressure: It is for your benefit. It can motivate you to protect yourself and those you love, inspire you to work harder, force you to organize your life, and even incite you to improve your interpersonal relationships. Just as it secretes ACTH into your system to protect and improve your body, it can inject a motivation into your spirit that by the grace of God will improve your spiritual life—if you will let it.

CHAPTER 6

The Bad News
About Pressure

It is impossible to herald the good news about pressure without implying that there is also bad news. You need to know how pressure operates so that you can avoid its harmful features.

You live in a pressurized age, and you have known this all your life. A recent survey indicated that 82 percent of the population felt they needed less stress in their daily lives. Most doctors attribute the following statistics to the real or imagined stress confronting people today:

• More than 230 million prescriptions for tranquilizers were filled last year.

• More than one million people have heart attacks each year.

• One of ten Americans is an alcoholic.

• It is estimated that 8 million people have ulcers.

• Some 25 million people have high blood pressure.

• Stress-related mental disorders account for a $17 billion decline in productivity annually.

• More than $60 billion has been lost due to stress-related physical disorders.

• Protracted stress can weaken a person's natural defense mechanism, lowering his resistance and making him vulnerable to pneumonia, tuberculosis, polio, and other communicable diseases.

• Between 1940 and 1950, heart attacks increased 23 percent and the rate is still rising.

• One in five Americans will experience a heart attack before age sixty.

• American doctors have conquered or learned to control polio, tuberculosis, and many communicable diseases, but the No. 1 killer is still heart attack, and the No. 1 cause is pressure-produced stress.

Unquestionably, pressure-produced stress can have a devastating effect on a person's health. Even before stress research became popular, doctors taught us that "emotionally induced illness" accounts for 65 to 85 percent of all sickness today. In the United States, where patients from all walks of life have access to the finest in medical attention, we can assume the factor is close to 85 percent. Think of the unnecessary sickness, suffering, and premature death that can be blamed on emotional illness.

More beneficial than any medical program would be a national stress reduction program. However, stress reduction must come either from God or from resources within a person. Very little can be accomplished in adults by other people.

MIND OVER BODY

It is no accident of fate that the mind is placed within the head of the body and rules over the whole. This was part of our Creator's ingenious design. The human mind, which has long fascinated mankind, is even today the least understood organ of the body. Medical science has much to learn about this incredible mechanism, and all agree that it is the most complex organism in the world.

As the mind goes, so goes the body. If you have a healthy mind, you will extend the natural health of your body. If you have an unhealthy mind, it will soon impair the rest of you. This may explain why the soul was often equated by the ancients with the mind. "Soul" means "life," and the mind determines life, be it lifestyle, philosophy, health, or mental attitude toward the pressure-producing circumstances of life.

A study of pressure and stress would not be complete without at least a casual examination of the mind. The more we understand its function, the easier it is for us to cooperate with it. Consider the following diagram:

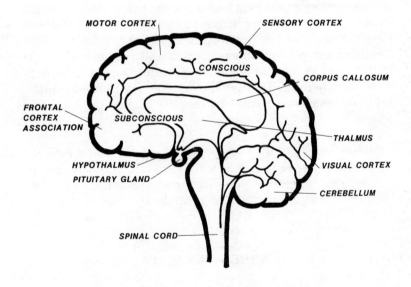

The brain contains these intricate organs and many others, all of which play a role in the psychophysiologic (mind-body) reaction to pressure described in the preceding chapter. The brain also houses the conscious and the subconscious mind. Both influence the body's reactions to pressure.

Two stress researchers describe the brain's impact this way:

> The primary stress response is the fight or flight response. This reaction has helped ensure our survival and continues to do so; no amount of relaxation training can ever diminish the intensity of this innate reflex. Stress is physical, intended to enable a physical response to a physical threat; however, *any* threat— physical or symbolic—can bring about this response. Once the stimulation of the event penetrates the psychological defenses, the body prepares for action. Increased hormonal secretion, cardiovascular activity, and energy supply signify a state of stress, a state of extreme readiness to act as soon as the voluntary control centers decide the form of the action, which in our social situation is often no "action" at all. Usually the threat is not real, but holds only symbolic significance. Our lives are not in danger, only our egos. Physical action is not warranted and must be subdued, but for the body organs it is too late: what took only minutes to start will take hours to undo. The stress products are flowing through the system and will activate various organs until they are reabsorbed back into storage or gradually used by the body. And while this gradual process is taking place, the body organs suffer.[1]

The key word in all stress literature is *time*. As a rule of thumb, we can usually measure the effects of pressure-produced stress in terms of time and know whether it will be harmful or helpful. Negative stress can be helpful when the body fulfills its ability to adapt to a situation. But when the same pressure is experienced over a long period of time, it can overload the system and cause serious maladies. Every person is different, and we do not share similar tolerances. Consequently some people can absorb more pressure than others; but ultimately we all have our own breaking points.

Fright probably offers the clearest illustration of this principle. Every person has a built-in fright alarm system. If your doorbell rings unexpectedly at 3:00 A.M., your hypothalmus gland—a kind of first sergeant for your entire autonomic nervous system—activates the endocrine system, particularly the

---

[1]Daniel A. Girdano and George S. Everly, Jr., *Controlling Stress and Tension: A Holistic Approach* (Englewood Cliffs, N.J.: Prentice-Hall, Inc., 1979), 25.

pituitary gland, which in turn arouses all the other glands and organs of the body. Probably the most important of these endocrine glands are the adrenals, which lie atop the kidneys. They secrete adrenalin, which instantly alerts your entire body for flight or fight. By this time your metabolism has speeded up, your heartbeat is racing, and your red blood cell count has increased, delivering more oxygen to your cells for greater energy.

All this activity takes place in a split second, allowing you to bound out of bed mentally alert. Feeling threatened or at least wary, you may open your drawer, reach for your gun, and then carefully check the front door. When you are relieved to find that the Western Union boy is simply trying to deliver a telegram to your next-door neighbor, you climb back into bed, hoping to renew your pattern of sleep. Wrong! You lie there wide-eyed, your activated system unable to relax for a long time—until about ten minutes before the alarm clock rings.

Except for the loss of sleep, this emergency activity is almost never harmful to a normally healthy person (although it could prove fatal to a chronic heart patient). Ordinarily the body's flushing system gradually absorbs or expels the ACTH, or fright-alarm fluid, without damage to the system. In fact, the experience may well have toned up your entire system.

This is not the case with regard to protracted worry, self-pity, revenge, hostility, and other tension-producing reactions to the pressures of life. For example, suppose your job is in jeopardy, you feel guilty about not tithing the past few months, and your money runs out before all the bills are paid. You cannot reduce your expenses or find a better job, so as far as you can see ahead, there is no hope. Whether you realize it or not, First Sergeant Hypothalamus barks out the orders to the autonomous nervous system, which starts to upset such involuntary organs as the liver, heart, and kidneys. This activates the pituitary and endocrine system and the adrenals, pumping ACTH through your system with all the previously mentioned responses—not as excessively as with fright, but for a longer period of time. At first your absorption and expulsion systems can function, but soon they are so overloaded that you become ill. Your body will break down at its point of least resistance.

Dr. Selye warns, "In the body, as in a chain, the weakest link breaks down under stress although all parts are equally exposed to it."[2] The hypothalmus gland has been compared to a first sergeant. It controls every organ of the body. If he becomes alerted, he sends a signal to all the other organs, and they become tense. If the tension is retained too long and if too much ACTH accumulates in the system, something will break down—at your point of least resistance. It may be a kidney, the lining of the stomach or gall bladder, or an important blood vessel in the brain.

Younger people enjoy the elasticity of youth. Consequently the body may exhibit few lasting effects of protracted tension and excessive amounts of ACTH. As the body matures, it becomes more brittle and vulnerable.

Dr. S. I. McMillen penned a classic that profoundly affected me in the early days of my counseling ministry. He pointed out that the adrenal glands generated tension throughout the body when activated. If protracted, such tension can trigger as many as fifty-one diseases, most of them common maladies. For example, he lists ulcers of the mouth, stomach, and intestines, ulcerative and mucous colitis, loss of appetite, hiccups, constipation, diarrhea, arteriosclerosis, coronary thrombosis, rheumatic fever, cerebral strokes of apoplexy, painful menstruation, painful coitus, frequent and painful urination, impotence, headaches of several types, epilepsy, psychoneuroses, senile dementia, hyperthyroidism, diabetes, asthma, backache, pain and spasm of muscles, osteoarthritis, infectious mononucleosis, polio, many (or all) infections, glaucoma, and psoriasis.[3]

THREE STAGES OF PROLONGED PRESSURE

We have already mentioned the three stages of stress observed by Dr. Selye: (1) alarm reaction; (2) resistance; and

---

[2]Selye, *Sress Without Distress*, 35.

[3]S. I. McMillen, *None of These Diseases* (Old Tappan, N.J.: Fleming H. Revell, 1963), 61–62.

(3) exhaustion. The following chart based on his study illustrates these:

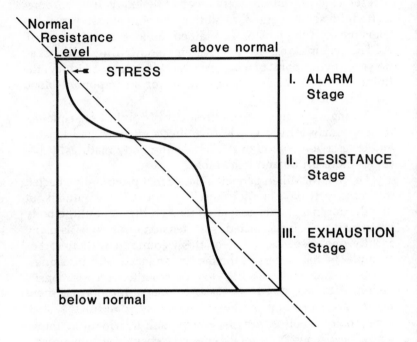

We are now familiar with the first two stages, alarm reaction and resistance. The third stage is extremely important. Even short-term stress will produce an exhaustion stage, just to give the body time to recuperate from the extra energy it expends. But if the pressure is prolonged, a person will remain in the exhaustion stage, which could eventually prove fatal.

Exhaustion does not always lead to death, though at that point life may hang by a fragile thread. You may remember the often-repeated television clip of former President Jimmy Carter, who fainted from exhaustion while jogging in a marathon. Although very weak and vulnerable at that time, he did indeed recuperate to serve the nation for many months.

The human body has an amazing ability to recover from exhaustion, but even this capability has a limit. According to

Dr. Selye, our G.A.S. (General Adaptation Syndrome), which provides the human body with its great adaptability, is finite. It is possible to so deplete this restoration capability that death ensues. Based on years of research Dr. Selye explains,

> Our reserves of adaptation energy could be compared to an inherited fortune from which we can make withdrawals; but there is no proof that we can also make additional deposits. We can squander our adaptability recklessly, "burning the candle at both ends," or we can learn to make this valuable resource last long, by using it wisely and sparingly, only for things that are worthwhile and cause least distress.

> As I have said, we have no objective proof that additional deposits of adaptation energy can be made beyond that inherited from our parents. Yet, everyone knows from personal experience that, after complete exhaustion by excessively stressful work during the day, a good night's sleep—and, after even more severe exhaustion, a few weeks of restful holidays—can restore our resistance and adaptability very close to what it was before. I said "very close to," because complete restoration is probably impossible, since every biologic activity leaves some irreversible "chemical scars." . . .[4]

Selye then distinguishes between "superficial" and "deep" adaptation energy. "Superficial" energy is readily available for short-term pressure experiences such as fear/fright, the baby born at night in the mountains, or jogging fatigue. Like money in a bank account, one simply writes a check and an energy payment becomes available immediately.

"Deep" adaptation energy is a stored reserve like an inherited fortune: When it's gone, it's gone. Selye allows that in some instances this reserve can be partially replenished, but that even then one's capacity to draw on this deep reservoir is definitely limited. As with our savings account, if no means is found to replenish it, withdrawals will eventually deplete one's inherited adaptive reserve, resulting in death.

> Still, after a lifetime of constant expenditure, even our last investments will be eventually exhausted if we only spend and never earn. I look upon the irreversible process of aging as something very similar. The stage of exhaustion, after a temporary demand upon the body, is reversible, but the complete exhaustion of all stores of deep adaptation energy is not; as these reserves are depleted, senility and, finally, death ensue.[5]

---

[4]Selye, *Stress Without Distress*, 28.
[5]Ibid., 29.

This condition explains why it is important either to reduce pressures as we grow older or to utilize the supernatural resources available to Christians in order to lessen their impact. Otherwise the deep, adaptive energy reserve will be used up prematurely.

Frank was a deacon in our church for almost four decades. In all the years I have been in the ministry, no man ever supported me during a time of crisis more than he. Needless to say, I loved him. About three months after his fifty-sixth wedding anniversary, Frank became ill; nine months later he died at the age of eighty. He and his wife Luella had no children, and only one relative was left to assist with the funeral arrangements. Frank died on a Thursday, and the funeral was planned for Monday. Luella, not in good health herself, was exhausted from nursing Frank for nine months. When he died, she could find no reason to live. While having coffee in the home with her relative on Saturday, she suddenly slumped over dead. Evidently her adaptive energy reserve was so depleted that when the pressure of severe grief produced a strong stress reaction, her account became bankrupt. Fortunately she was ready to meet the Lord—and her Frank—in heaven. The funeral for this dear couple was the only double funeral I have ever conducted.

SUMMARY

The human body's amazing ability to adapt to pressure is limited. I am convinced that Spirit-controlled Christians will make fewer demands on that deep reservoir of survival energy than non-Christians will. Consequently Christians should enjoy longer good health and life.

This does not mean that Christians will not face pressures of life. I have found that pressure is no respecter of persons. It strikes kings, dictators, presidents, the poor, the rich, the alcoholic, and the Spirit-controlled Christian. However, the intensity of the internalized pressure is less for the Christian, and his spiritual resources during times of potential stress should keep him from using up those precious reserves. Besides, there may be ways to replenish the reserves not yet discovered.

CHAPTER 7

How Pressure Affects Different People

People are different! Anyone who says that "all men are created equal" doesn't know what he is talking about.[1] When my seven-foot-two friend Ralph Drollinger, former basketball player for Athletes in Action, talks to me, at five-foot-seven, he usually sits on a chair or the table, and even then I have to look up at him. Can you imagine a one-on-one contest between us on the basketball court?

Nor do I possess the artistic ability to draw any of the diagrams or charts my creative mind can visualize. Untrained artists in my church used to paint or draw them for my public messages. I know five-year-old children who can draw better than I can. Why? It is a gift they are born with. Some people can sing, some can write music, and others can conceptualize, manufacture, produce, sell, or teach. Education can improve these gifts, but it will never create them.

I once interviewed a musician for the role of choir director for our church. He could arrange music and write songs, but he was not a pianist. By contrast, his wife played beautifully, particularly when using one of her husband's arrangements, yet she could neither arrange nor compose music. When I commented to my wife—the musician in our family—what an ex-

---

[1]The popular expression, derived from the Declaration of Independence, is a legal term meaning "all men are created equal under the law."

cellent pianist I thought the woman was, Bev responded, "But she is very mechanical; she doesn't feel her music."

Examining their temperaments, I discovered that the wife was the strong-willed choleric who as a child had set her mind to master the mechanics of the piano. She could play anything if given time to rehearse, but she didn't "feel" music. Her husband, who was predominantly melancholy in temperament, didn't play well, but he could hear and feel music even without the piano. Those are temperament traits one is born with, and they play a prominent role in how one responds to pressure.

Sir William Osler, an astute physician who lived before the modern pressures of life made heart attacks the No. 1 killer in our society, made this observation:

> It is not the delicate, neurotic person who has angina, . . . but the robust, the vigorous in mind and body, the keen and ambitious man, the indicator of whose engine is always at "full speed ahead" . . . the well-set man of from forty-five to fifty-five years of age, with military bearing, iron gray hair, and florid complexion.[2]

Basically he was talking about the hero of modern industry, the corporate executive, foreman, police sergeant, manager, or any competitive person.

My friend Harry is a national leader among the New York Life Insurance agents. "Competition" is his middle name! We used to play handball and racquetball before it was popular. One day, catching me out of shape and out of practice, he simply overpowered me. In three games I didn't earn more than five points! Afterward at lunch he gave me a copy of the best-selling book *Type A Behavior and Your Heart*, commenting, "This is the most important book I've read this year. I think you should read it." Before going to sleep that night, I perused the book and decided two things: (1) Harry loved me; and (2) he was concerned about my health.[3]

---

[2]McQuade and Aikman, *Stress*, 23.

[3]Meyer Friedman and Ray H. Rosenman, *Type A Behavior and Your Heart* (New York: Fawcett Crest, 1974).

That year my life resembled an accelerating merry-go-round. The book inspired me to (1) get in shape again; (2) delegate responsibilities better; (3) relax more; and (4) quit taking on more projects than I could fulfill properly.

Type A Behavior and Your Heart has become a basic resource for all authors and researchers on stress behavior and pressure. In their book *Stress,* McQuade and Aikman offer interesting background material on the book and its helpful teachings.

> Twenty years ago these two cardiologists were deep in the study of the standard heart risk factors: cigarette smoking, blood pressure, diet, obesity, and in particular serum cholesterol. Like cardiologists then—and now—their principal emphasis was on the build-up of fatty acids in the blood, which can eventually harden in the artery walls, narrowing the channel and keeping blood from the heart itself. Friedman says now, "I was cholesterol-oriented because I am a laboratory man and cholesterol does produce disease in animals. It was also something we could work on. So we thought, 'Let's get cholesterol down.'"
>
> Nevertheless, puzzling factors kept cropping up—among them the low incidence of heart disease in American women. Friedman points out, "Although American women seem to be protected from heart trouble, Mexican women have as much heart disease as their men. It is also one to one in Southern Italy, but it is four to one in Northern Italy. An American Negress in Chicago or North Carolina has more heart disease than her husband. Therefore it can't be sexual hormones. As a good scientist—my definition of a good scientist is one who looks at the exception—I should have connected. But I didn't think it through."
>
> One day in the early 1950s an upholsterer came in to redo the Friedman-Rosenman waiting room, and was puzzled by the condition of the chairs. The only place the chairs were worn, he said, was at the front edge of the seats. This Dr. Friedman interprets today as an indication that "Our individual patients were signaling us. Over 90 percent were showing signs of struggle in their lives."
>
> From these simple beginnings came a program that was to involve thousands of staff hours and hundreds of thousands of research dollars during the succeeding two decades. The result is an impressive case for the idea that stress and behavior are principal culprits in the high incidence of heart attacks among middle-age Americans; that personality patterns are of vital importance; and—perhaps—that these personality patterns can be changed before it is too late. . . .

Then came a study with accountants which involved more than opinion, and which began to attract considerable attention. Accountants were chosen for the study because their work rises and falls in intensity, alternating spells of easy routine with periods such as tax time when everyone knocks himself out to meet a deadline. All were asked to keep detailed diaries of what they ate, and Friedman and Rosenman arranged to examine each twice a month, measuring cholesterol levels during both slack periods and times of heavy pressure.

Two significant cholesterol peaks occurred: first, when the accountants were closing out the yearly books of their clients in January, and again in March to mid-April when they were heavily involved in preparing income tax returns. Not everyone reacted to the stress in the same degree, but there was an overall jump of fatty acids in the blood during these periods, with a falling off in months of more placid work. The correlation between work loads and cholesterol readings was direct, and was independent of individual variations in diet, weight, or amount of exercise.

At the same time they were studying the accountants, Friedman and Rosenman also began considering the matter of individual differences in temperament that might influence people's reactions to stress. No two individuals handle stress identically, but which one ends up with heart disease and which one doesn't?

"Thus emerged our Type A and Type B," says Rosenman.

Type A, either male or female, is characterized by intense drive, aggressiveness, ambition, competitiveness, pressure for getting things done, and the habit of pitting himself against the clock. He may give an impression of iron control, or wear a mask of easy geniality, but the strain glints through.

By contrast, Type B's manner is more genuinely easy. He is open. He is not always glancing at his watch. He is not so preoccupied with achievement, is less competitive, and even speaks in a more modulated style.

Most people are mixtures of Type A and Type B, of course, and Rosenman and Friedman have sharpened their interviewing techniques to the point where they recognize four distinct subdivisions of each group, ranging from A-1, the most virulent, down to B-4, the mildest.[4]

McQuade and Aikman provide a helpful synopsis of Friedman and Rosenman's Type A and B personalities.

---

[4]McQuade and Aikman, *Stress*, 23–26.

The general picture that emerges of the two types is familiar, recognizable—and a bit broad. The extreme Type A is the man who, while waiting to see the dentist, is on the telephone making business calls. He speaks in staccato, and has a tendency to end his sentences in a rush. He frequently sighs faintly between words (Dr. Friedman identifies this as "deadly—a sign of emotional exhaustion"). Type A is seldom out of his office or shop sick. He rarely goes to a doctor, and almost never to a psychiatrist—he does not feel he needs either. Indeed many Type A's die of otherwise recoverable coronaries simply because they wait too long to call for help. When necessity does force an A into a physician's hands, he is an impatient patient. One malady which is rather unlikely to strike him is peptic ulcer.

Type A is often a little hard to get along with. His chuckle is rather grim. He does not drive people who work under him as hard as he drives himself, but he has little time to waste with them. He wants respect, not affection. Yet in some ways he can be said to be more sensitive than the milder Type B. He hates to fire anyone and will go to great lengths to avoid it. Sometimes the only way he can resolve such a situation is by mounting a general office crisis. If he himself has ever been fired it is not for underachievement but probably because of a personality clash with a colleague or superior.

Type A, surprisingly, goes to bed earlier than Type B. He doesn't get much out of home life anyway, and might as well prepare for the day ahead with a good night's rest, whereas Type B will get interested in something and sit up late, or simply socialize. Type A smokes cigarettes, never a pipe. Headwaiters learn not to keep him waiting for a reservation; if they do, they lose him. They like him because he doesn't linger over his meals, and doesn't complain about the cooking. He salts the meal before he tastes it, and has never sent a bottle of wine back to the cellar.

Type A's have little time for exercise. When they do play golf it is fast through, and in tennis they can be difficult partners. On vacation they like to go to lively, competitive places and if possible to combine the vacation with business. They never return to work a day or two late; they are more likely to be back early. Most days they stay on at the office well into the evening, and when they do leave, their desk tops are clear.

But in the competition for the top jobs in their companies, says Dr. Friedman, A's often lose out to B's. They lose because they are *too* competitive—narrowly, compulsively so. They make decisions too fast—in minutes, instead of days—and so may make serious business mistakes. They are intoxicated by numerical competition: how many units sold in Phoenix, how many miles traveled in February. Life to an A-1 is a race against a clock and an adding machine. He lives by numbers in a constant effort to build up higher totals.[5]

According to Dr. Friedman, "The great salesmen are A's. The corporation presidents are usually B's." Rosenman adds,

> What is most tragic of all in this picture of hopeful, driving energy is that the Type A's are two or three times more likely than the Type B's to get coronary heart disease in middle age. In all of Sinclair Lewis's pitiless characterizations of American businessmen there is nothing so devastating as these doctors' cool statistics.[6]

The results of all this indicates that Type A people (men or women) are more likely than others to suffer heart attacks. Of 3,500 patients they studied aged thirty-one to fifty-nine with no known history of heart disease, 257 developed coronary heart trouble, 70 percent of them Type A's. Unless a Type A person changes his lifestyle by reducing his external pressures, he is more likely to experience heart difficulties with each passing year.

TEMPERAMENT: YOU'RE BORN WITH IT

Many theories of human behavior are prevalent today: Introvert/extrovert; I'm OK, you're OK; and many others. I have found the theory of the four temperaments to be the best explanation of why we act the way we do. Certainly it is the oldest on record. In fact, it exists in embryo in the Bible, for the writer of Proverbs 30:11–14 (ASV) discerned four kinds of people. About seven hundred years later Hippocrates, the father of medicine, observed four types of people whom he labeled Sanguine, Choleric, Melancholy, and Phlegmatic.

For 2,300 years the four temperaments theory of human behavior was dominant until the advancement of modern psychology and its notion that all people were born neutral. This was based on the unscientific theory of evolution, which identifies men as animals originating from a common source with other animals. During the past decade or so, both the

---

[5]Ibid., 26–28.
[6]Ibid., 28.

theory of evolution and its offspring, the study of psychology, have fallen on hard times, because so many of their changing theories have been disproven. In addition, biologists have become increasingly aware that a certain degree of every person's behavior is born in him (estimates range from 10 percent to as high as 20 percent). This new field of research, called sociobiology, may just lead to the return to popularity of the theory of the four temperaments. An increasing number of anthropologists, biologists, and behaviorists are admitting that certain characteristics seem to be part of one's personality from birth.

INGREDIENTS OF BEHAVIOR

A set theory of human behavior is difficult to tie down, because so many ingredients play a part and because people are different; moreover, variant ingredients in life change as the individual matures. The following formula governs the most prominent causes of human behavior.

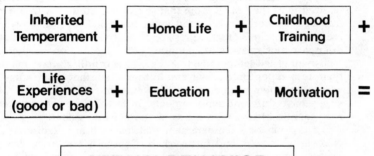

Your inherited temperament, the most basic of the raw materials from which your behavior is drawn, is determined largely through the genes from your parents and grandparents. Their nationality and race are a vital factor, for temperaments follow basic nationality lines. I had long observed the various temperaments of Europeans from German cholerics to sanguine/melancholy Italians. On a trip around the world, my wife and I visited forty-two countries. One of the most intriguing of observations was the indomitable spirit of the Polish people compared with the more passive drives of some of the other Eastern European satellite countries (and this was five years before Solidarity union was formed). Another observation was the high percentage of cholerics among some of the orientals, particularly the Japanese; the choleric/melancholies among the Chinese; and choleric/phlegmatics of the Koreans as compared with the sanguine/phlegmatic or phlegmatic/sanguine temperaments of many of the African nationalities. Orientals tend to be serious workaholics, while many of the Africans are prone to be emotional, spontaneous people. These characteristics seem to follow them even when they migrate to our country and adopt a new way of life.

WHAT IS TEMPERAMENT?

Temperament is the combination of traits we inherited from our parents. No one knows where it resides, but personally I think it is somewhere in the mind or emotional center (often referred to as the *heart*). From that source it combines with other human characteristics to produce our basic makeup. Most of us are more conscious of its expression than we are its function. For example, sports lovers are familiar with the Selmon brothers, whose inherited temperament and physical condition have made them into super football players. In their case, they share somewhat similar temperaments, but it often seems that brothers and sisters have different temperaments. In fact, I have seldom met even identical twins with the same basic temperament.

It is a person's temperament that makes him outgoing and extrovertish or shy and introvertish. Doubtless you know both kinds of people who were born to the same parents. Similarly, it is temperament that makes some people art and music enthusiasts while others are sports or industry minded. In fact, I have met outstanding musicians whose brothers were tone deaf. There comes to mind one professional football player whose brother has never watched him play a game because, as he tells it, he "just can't stand to watch violence."

Temperament is not the only influence upon our behavior, of course, because early homelife, training, education, and motivation also exercise powerful influences on our actions throughout life. Temperament is, however, the number-one influence on a person's life, not only because it is the first thing that affects us but because, like body structure, color of eyes, and other physical characteristics, it escorts us through life. An extrovert is an extrovert—he may tone down the expression of his extroversion, but he will always be an extrovert. Similarly, although an introvert may be able to come out of his shell and act more aggressively, he will never be transformed into an extrovert. Temperament sets broad guidelines on everyone's behavior—patterns which will influence a person as long as he lives. On the one side are his strengths, on the other his weaknesses. The primary advantage to learning about the four basic temperaments is to discover your most pronounced strengths and weaknesses so that with God's help you can overcome your weaknesses and take maximum advantage of your strengths. In this way you can fulfill your personal destiny.[7]

THE BLENDS OF TEMPERAMENT

A chief factor in complicating the theory of the four temperaments is that *no one is completely one temperament.* That may have been true in Hippocrates' day, when his countrymen were pure Greeks, but it is no longer true. Most people are nationality mixtures today. You can imagine what this has done to their original temperament! Mixed ancestry produces a blending of temperaments. For example, I am 50 percent Scottish, 25 percent French, and 25 percent Irish—each nationality having a different temperament.

As already indicated, some people have three temperaments—one predominant and two secondary. The most unusual case I have tested so far involves a close friend. Sometimes I thought he was a choleric; at other times his perfectionism suggested he was predominantly melancholy, though at other times he acted sanguine. He kept insisting, "I am predominantly sanguine." But he was such a workaholic and "tiger" in his field that I could not agree. I only knew for sure that he was a strong extrovert. When he completed my temperament test, it all became clear: He scored 34 percent sanguine, 33 percent choleric, and 33 percent melancholy. That explains his extroversion (67 percent) and his fluctuations of mood.

My testing, however, indicates that finding three temperaments so equally balanced in one person is really quite rare. The vast majority of the fifteen thousand tests I have adminis-

[7]Tim LaHaye, *Understanding the Male Temperament* (Old Tappan, N.J.: Fleming H. Revell, 1977), 52–55.

tered show one predominant temperament; a 20–45 percent secondary one, and a third one that is minimal.

For our purposes in examining the effects of your temperament on the way you react to pressure, we will consider only the four temperaments. You can easily interpret the influence of your secondary temperament on your own.

THE SANGUINE TEMPERAMENT

Sparky Sanguine is a warm, buoyant, lively and "enjoying" person. He is receptive by nature, and external impressions easily find their way to his heart, where they readily cause an outburst of response. Feelings rather than reflective thoughts predominate to form his decisions. Sparky is so outgoing that I call him a superextrovert. Mr. Sanguine has an unusual capacity for enjoying himself and usually passes on his fun-loving spirit. The moment he enters a room he tends to lift the spirits of everyone present by his exuberant conversation. He is a fascinating storyteller, and his warm, emotional nature almost makes him relive the experience as he tells it.

Mr. Sanguine never lacks for friends. As one writer noted, "His naive, spontaneous, genial nature opens doors and hearts to him." He can genuinely feel the joys and sorrows of the person he meets and has the capacity to make him feel important, as though he were a very special friend—and he *is* as long as he is looking at you or until he fixes his eyes with equal intensity on the next person he meets. The Sanguine has what I call "hanging eyes." That is, his eyes hang or "fix" on you until he loses interest in you or someone else comes along to attract his attention.

The Sanguine is never at a loss for words, though he often speaks without thinking. His open sincerity, however, has a disarming effect on many of his listeners, causing them to respond to his mood. His freewheeling, seemingly exciting, extrovertish way of life makes him the envy of the more timid temperament types. . . .

Sparky Sanguine enjoys people and detests solitude. He is at his best surrounded by friends where he is the life of the party. He has an endless repertoire of interesting stories which he tells dramatically, making him a favorite with children as well as adults. This trait usually gains him admission at the best parties or social gatherings.

His noisy, blustering, friendly ways make him appear more confident than he really is, but his energy and lovable disposition get him by the rough spots of life. People have a way of excusing his weaknesses by saying, "That's just the way he is."[8]

---

[8]Ibid., 57–58.

SANGUINES AND PRESSURE

Sanguines rarely get ulcers; they usually give them to everyone else. Since people are a major cause of pressure and sanguines love to be around people, they are never far from pressure, which usually they have created.

These light-hearted people are often very disorganized, generally arrive late for meetings, and are rarely prepared for whatever they are supposed to do. I have watched sanguine songleaders select the songs for an evening service while walking down the aisle of the church. Despite their lack of preparation, they usually do a creditable job because they exude so much charisma. Sanguines are such good actors and people responders that they often do a better job on the platform than other temperaments who prepare carefully. One can't help but wonder how effective sanguines could be if they would only learn to plan for whatever lies ahead. Unfortunately each time they "get by" with improvising under pressure, they learn that advance planning is not really crucial for success.

This could be the reason why sanguines are often "short-termers." That is, they run out of material after a time and must move on to their next job. Sanguine preachers, for example, usually stay in a church for only two or three years. Pressure tends to drive them to the golf course rather than to the study.

Because they are prone to be late, undependable, undisciplined, and unprepared, sanguines are never far from pressure. Can you visualize the personable, people-oriented homemaker who welcomes the neighbor in for a "fifteen-minute coffee klatsch," only to talk too long and discover that the party has ended only minutes before her husband is due home? She furiously whips through the house, trying frantically to set things in order for his arrival. Dinner is late, the house is a mess, and she is not prepared for his sarcastic insults; she lashes out in self-defense about her "overworked schedule" or "the pressures of three small children." Such reactions do little for a loving relationship.

Sanguines are quick of speech and often use their vocal chords to defend themselves when pressed. More aggressive types learn that in verbally attacking other people they can often intimidate them into submission, so they cover their mistakes by pressurizing others. I know one sanguine who reminds me of the Saint Bernard dog we once had. After knocking me down at the front gate and breaking my glasses, he put both paws on my shoulders and licked my face. Even though you are right in a disagreement with a sanguine, he will attack you and bluster, and when you leave, you have failed to confront him with the problem. In fact, he has made you feel that it was all your fault for bringing up the matter in the first place.

Women sanguines are often screamers. That is, their frustration is never far from the surface, so they scream at their children, husband, neighbor, or whoever is near. Male sanguines tend to talk too loudly, making demands or speaking more dogmatically than their grasp of the facts would allow. If one gives a sanguine enough rope, he will usually hang himself verbally.

One of the most uncomplimentary tendencies of a sanguine under pressure is his difficulty in honestly taking the blame for his mistakes. Because he commands a giant ego, needs the love and admiration of others, and lacks discipline, it is easy for him to pass the buck, blame others for his mistakes, and in some cases lie to get out of a trap. This is why parents of sanguine children need to concentrate on teaching them self-discipline and truth-telling. Otherwise they will develop a flexible conscience.

Some sanguines resort to weepy repentance when confronted with the pressure caused by their unkempt ways. Such repentance is usually short-lived; the sanguine has learned little or nothing from experience.

Sanguines are easily intimidated by more forceful, cruel personalities. I have seen many highly emotional wives, with tremendous capacities to love and be loved, become distraught because their husbands cold-bloodedly used their quest for self-acceptance to browbeat them into taking the blame for anything that goes wrong. It always pains me to hear a woman cry, "I know it is all my fault," when that is rarely the case. One woman was intimidated into accepting her husband's infidelity because he convinced her she was inadequate in bed; actually he acted immorally because he was sinful.

Lying never solves anything. The Bible enjoins us, "Let

every man speak truth with his neighbor" and "Lying brings a snare" (see Eph. 4:25; Prov. 29:25). It takes sanguines a long time to learn that it is much easier to face those unpleasant pressures of life squarely, take full responsibility for mistakes, and then do two things: (1) solve the present difficulty; and (2) learn from the experience.

Most sanguines cannot endure emotional pressure very long. They will start talking, tell an unrelated joke, or run away from the problem. An example of this occurred in the rental car of a nationally famous minister in January 1980. Twelve of us had breakfast with former President Carter and asked several questions: Why did he not oppose abortion? Why had he endorsed the Equal Rights Amendment in view of the harm it would do to the family? Why did he refuse to support a voluntary school prayer amendment for our public schools? Five of us drove out of the White House grounds in deep silence. I was very depressed by what I had heard, and so were the others. Suddenly the most sanguine of the group split the silence with an unrelated and rather bizarre joke. He was reacting naturally to the emotional pressures that he felt at the moment.

As we have noted, sanguines often give ulcers to others because they will not face their problems and do something constructive about them. A sanguine manager, administrator, or minister, for instance, has an interesting way of trying to solve personnel problems. If he senses another's displeasure, he will tactfully take him out for coffee, lunch, or an evening of entertainment. He will rarely discuss the problem, preferring to use his charismatic charm to disarm his friend's hostility or displeasure. He leaves that encounter feeling that he has solved his problem, whereas in reality he has only delayed judgment day for a while. As a husband he will bring home a "peace offering" or "take the family out to dinner" to solve a problem, but as you know, that only relieves the immediate pressure; it does not really change anything. If only he would face issues realistically and do something about them, he would reduce most of his life pressures.

Because sanguines cannot tolerate the discomfort of pressure, they always react in some way: An explosive outburst, tears, jokes, lies, change of subject, or "fellowship." They cannot suffer pressure in silence. Fortunately their happy disposition easily forgets unpleasant circumstances; the first moving object or person that catches their eye gains their attention, and they mentally or physically separate themselves from the cause of their pressure temporarily. If sanguines could learn to use pressure as motivation toward problem-solving, their lives would be greatly enriched, and I believe they would be 25-to-50 percent more successful in their chosen fields.

THE CHOLERIC TEMPERAMENT

Rocky Choleric is the hot, quick, active, practical, and strong-willed temperament type which is self-sufficient and very independent. He tends to be decisive and opinionated, finding it easy to make decisions both for himself and [for] other people. Like Sparky Sanguine, Rocky Choleric is an extrovert, but not nearly so intense.

Mr. Choleric thrives on activity. In fact, to him, "life is activity." He does not need to be stimulated by his environment, but rather stimulates his environment with his endless ideas, plans, goals, and ambitions. He does not engage in aimless activity, for he has a practical, keen mind, capable of making sound, instant decisions or planning worthwhile projects. He does not vacillate under the pressure of what others think, but takes a definite stand on issues and can often be found crusading against some social injustice or subversive situation.

Rocky is not frightened by adversities; in fact, they tend to encourage him. His dogged determination usually allows him to succeed where others have failed, not because his plans are better than theirs, but because others have become discouraged and quit, whereas he has doggedly kept pushing ahead. If there is any truth to the adage that leaders are born, not made, then he is a natural-born leader, what business management experts call the SNL (Strong Natural Leader).

Mr. Choleric's emotional nature is the least developed part of his temperament. He does not sympathize easily with others, nor does he naturally show or express compassion. He is often embarrassed or disgusted by the tears of others and is usually insensitive to their needs. Reflecting little appreciation for music and the fine arts, unless his secondary temperament traits are those of the Melancholy, he primarily seeks utilitarian and productive values in life.

The Choleric is quick to recognize opportunities and equally as quick to diagnose the best ways to make use of them. He has a well-organized mind, though details usually bore him. Not given to analysis, but rather to quick, almost intuitive appraisal, he tends to look at the goal for which he is working without recognizing the potential pitfalls and obstacles in the path. Once he has started toward his goal, he may run roughshod over individuals who stand in his way. He tends to be domineering and bossy and does not hesitate to use people to accomplish his ends. He is often considered an opportunist. . . .

Any profession that requires leadership, motivation, and productivity is open to a Choleric, provided it does not require too much attention to details and analytical planning. Committee meetings and long-range planning bore him, for he is a doer. . . .

Rocky is a developer by nature. When he and his wife drive through the countryside, he cannot share her enjoyment of the "beautiful rolling hillsides," for he envisions road graders carving out streets and builders constructing homes, schools, and shopping centers. Most of today's cities and suburbs were first envisioned by a Choleric. . . .

Rocky Choleric is a natural motivator of other people. He oozes self-confidence, is extremely goal-conscious, and can inspire others to envision his goals. Consequently, his associates may find themselves more productive by following his lead. His primary weakness as a leader is that he is hard to please and tends to run roughshod over other people. If he only knew how others look to him for approval and encouragement, he would spend more time patting them on the back and acknowledging their accomplishments—which would generate even greater dedication from his colleagues. The problem is, however, the Choleric subconsciously thinks that approval and encouragement will lead to complacency, and he assumes that an employee's productivity will fall off if he is too complimentary. Thus he will resort to criticism and faultfinding, in the hope that this will inspire greater effort. Unfortunately, he must learn that criticism is a *de*motivator. Once Rocky discovers that people require reassurance and stimulation in order to perform at the height of their potential, his role as leader will radically improve.[9]

CHOLERICS UNDER PRESSURE

No one can create more pressure than a choleric. He thrives on it—until his body breaks down with ulcers, high blood pressure, heart attack, or other physical adversities. We have already examined the Type A personality, so we are somewhat prepared for the choleric man or woman. Actually, a classic Type A is a choleric/melancholy combination.

---

[9]Ibid., 64–67.

Some of the choleric's high pressure quotient is occasioned by his "god complex." Perhaps it would be better to label it an "omnipotence complex." Cholerics are always overinvolved. They are willing to tackle anything that needs to be done. They never ask, "Why doesn't someone else do something about this?" To almost any need they respond, "Let's get organized and put the troops to work!" Then they start barking orders to others.

Cholerics rarely get depressed when a project fails, because they have thirty other irons in the fire to keep their overly active minds occupied. Instead of wallowing in self-pity over an insult, failure, or rejection, they busy themselves with their next project.

However, this penchant for taking on more than anyone could possibly accomplish often proves to be the cause of greatest pressures. Cholerics are extremely goal-oriented, but unless their secondary temperament is melancholy, they will not be adept at planning, analyzing, and detailing. In fact, they usually don't like it. Cholerics are doers. Consequently they may rush into battle before establishing a plan of attack, thus creating a great deal of pressure.

Many of the frenetic activities of the choleric should be put on a back burner. He is successful in the business world, not because his ideas are so well designed, but because he launches them while others are still determining theirs. Some of his better notions die on the drawing board, for a choleric has usually implemented his ideas and projects before he realizes that a better way exists. However, dogged determination stands him in good stead, for he usually finishes what he starts.

The choleric typically responds to pressure by refusing to give up. When he encounters an impossible situation, he glibly retorts, "Nothing is impossible." A choleric I know contends, "I never take no for an answer unless I hear it eight or ten times." Even then he is apt to press doggedly onward. Pressure discourages some people, but not the choleric; it simply serves as grist for his mill. Thriving on opposition, in some cases he will clench his teeth and press on regardless. At other times his creative mind will envision a crafty device to achieve his ends. It may not be legal, honest, or fair, but that doesn't always deter him.

Because of their penchant for adopting excessive loads and their natural inability to delegate responsibility, cholerics tend to take their extra time away from the family. Their ten-hour days soon increase to twelve and fifteen hours, the day off becomes another working day, and vacation time never seems to arrive. Consequently the family suffers.

Interpersonal relationships are not a choleric's strength, and work pressures compound this. He tends to be impatient with those less motivated than himself, critical and demanding of others, even unappreciative of people when they do well. If he is an employer, he usually experiences a high turnover at his place of business. His family members tend to give him a wide berth. Cruel and unkind by nature, he can be very cutting and sarcastic under pressure. Unless he seeks the help of God and walks in the Spirit, he will be prone to leave many damaged psyches and wounded egos in his wake. One choleric supervisor was reported to be "very productive, but leaves a trail of weepy subordinates." Gentle spirits should think twice before getting involved with cholerics.

The choleric's principal weapon is his tongue. No one can use it with greater dexterity and brutality. Because he enjoys pressure, he delights in heaping it upon others. His motto: "We do better under pressure."

Cholerics need to understand that there is more to life than money, success, or even accomplishment. Jesus said, "Man's life consists not in the things which he possesses" and "What shall it profit a man if he gain the whole world and lose his own soul?" (see Luke 12:15; Matt. 16:26). Mr. or Mrs. Pressure-building Choleric may successfully launch projects, develop businesses, and construct churches—all to the benefit of others—but if such endeavors succeed at the expense of their relationsip with spouse, children, parents, and others, "What shall it profit?"

In short, a choleric must establish the best priorities for his life and concentrate on them. A man without priorities may become engrossed in activities that may better have been left alone. The choleric needs to set his priorities in this order:

1. God
2. Wife
3. Family
4. Vocation

Then he needs to establish clearly defined goals, rejecting creative ideas that do not contribute to the realization of these goals. He also must develop a love for people, learning to encourage others and become interested in them. His time spent on people will be returned to him multiplied, because others will extend themselves in appreciation, thus relieving him of many of his pressures.

THE MELANCHOLY TEMPERAMENT

The melancholy is the richest temperament of all. He is

> . . . an analytical, self-sacrificing, gifted perfectionist type with a very sensitive emotional nature. No one gets more enjoyment from the fine arts than the melancholy. By nature, he is prone to be an introvert, but since his feelings predominate, he is given to a variety of moods. Sometimes they will lift him to heights of ecstasy that cause him to act more extroverted. However, at other times he will be gloomy and depressed, and during these periods he becomes withdrawn and can be quite antagonistic. This tendency toward black moods has earned him the reputation of being the "dark temperament."
>
> Mr. Melancholy is a very faithful friend, but unlike the sanguine, he does not make friends easily. He seldom pushes himself forward to meet people, but rather lets them come to him. He is perhaps the most dependable of all the temperaments, for his perfectionist tendencies do not permit him to be a shirker or let others down when they are counting on him. His natural reticence to put himself forward is not an indication that he doesn't enjoy people. Like the rest of us, he not only likes others but has a strong desire to be loved by them. Disappointing experiences make him reluctant to take people at face value; thus he is prone to be suspicious when others seek him out or shower him with attention.
>
> His exceptional analytical ability causes him to diagnose accurately the obstacles and dangers of any project he has a part in planning. This is in sharp contrast to the choleric, who rarely anticipates problems or difficulties, but is confident he can cope with whatever crises may arise. Such a characteristic often finds

the melancholy reticent to initiate some new project or in conflict with those who wish to do so. Whenever a person looks at obstacles instead of resources or goals, he will easily become discouraged before he starts. If you confront a melancholy about his pessimistic stage, he will usually retort, "I am not! I'm just being realistic." In other words, his usual thinking process makes him realistically pessimistic. Occasionally, in one of his exemplary moods of emotional ecstasy or inspiration, he may produce some great work of art or genius, but these accomplishments are often followed by periods of great depression.

Melancholies usually find their greatest meaning in life through personal sacrifice. They seem desirous of making themselves suffer and will often choose a difficult life vocation involving great personal sacrifice. But once it is chosen, they are prone to be very thorough and persistent in their pursuit of it and more than likely will accomplish great good if their natural tendency to gripe throughout the sacrificial process doesn't get them so depressed that they give up on it altogether. No temperament has so much natural potential when energized by the Holy Spirit as the melancholy.

As a general rule, no other temperament has a higher I.Q., creativity, or imagination than a melancholy, and no one else is as capable of perfectionism. Most of the world's great composers, artists, musicians, inventors, philosophers, theoreticians, theologians, scientists, and dedicated educators have been predominantly melancholies. Name a famous artist, composer, or orchestra leader and you have identified another genius (and often eccentric) melancholy. Consider Rembrandt, Van Gogh, Beethoven, Mozart, Wagner, and a host of others. Usually the greater the degree of genius, the greater will be the predominance of a melancholy temperament.

Any vocation that requires perfection, self-sacrifice, and creativity is open to a melancholy. However, he tends to place self-imposed limitations on his potential by underestimating himself and exaggerating obstacles. Almost any humanitarian vocation will attract melancholies to its staff. . . .

The analytical ability required to design buildings, lay out a landscape, or look at acreage and envision a cohesive development usually requires a melancholy temperament. In the building trades the melancholy may want to supervise construction. However, he would be better off hiring a project supervisor who works better with people—and then spend his own time on the drawing board. He becomes frustrated by the usual personnel problems and, with his unrealistic perfectionist demands, adds to them. . . .

All melancholies, of course, do not enter the professions or arts. Many become craftsmen of a high quality—finish carpenters, bricklayers, plumbers, plasterers, scientists, nurserymen, playwrights, authors, mechanics, engineers, and members of almost every profession that provides a meaningful service to humanity. One vocation that seems to attract the melancholy, surprisingly enough, is acting, for we tend to identify this profession with an extrovert. On stage, the melancholy can become another person and even adopt that personality, no matter how much extroversion it requires, but as soon as the play is over and he comes down from his emotional high, he reverts back to his own more introverted personality.[10]

MELANCHOLIES UNDER PRESSURE

Like everyone else, melancholies face pressure in life. But because of their sensitive, creative, and perfectionistic ways, everything in life is intensified, especially pressure. Probably no temperament bears more pressure in his heart and mind than does the melancholy. This may be why his mortality rate is approximately seven years lower than that of other types.

We have already seen that one's mental attitude can increase or decrease realistic pressure. That is bad news for a melancholy: One of his biggest problems in life relates to his mental attitude. A perfectionist by nature, he is extremely negative, critical, and suspicious—as critical of himself as he is of others.

One of a melancholy's consistent pressures is his desire to do everything perfectly. While commendable to a point, this trait can become maddening to others, for he often spends an inordinate amount of time on trivia or nonessentials at the neglect of more important matters. Sometimes he will neglect one assignment altogether until finishing a lesser project at 110-percent perfection level. Some melancholies cause pressure in their employer because they are perfection oriented rather than production oriented; consequently they don't produce enough to pay for their perfectionist productivity level.

Melancholy housewives and mothers are easily the best housekeepers and cooks. Dinner is always on time. But they may lack gracious flexibility. Woe to the child who tracks mud

---

[10]Ibid., 75–77.

over the freshly scrubbed kitchen floor! Or woe to the salesman husband who gets home late for dinner because he had to finalize that "big sale" at quitting time!

The melancholy's penchant for advance planning can drive the rest of the family off a cliff. Everything should be faithfully worried about. He often creates so much pressure contemplating and designing a vacation that all spontaneity and fun is eliminated.

Melancholies can worry themselves into pressure even when none exists. Most of the things they fear never materialize, but the pressure they build through worry is real. Such unnecessary fears often keep them from venturing out into something new, and as a result they build pressure through boredom, performing the same tasks repeatedly.

Since a melancholy person is predominantly an introvert, he will rarely externalize his pressures by angrily kicking things, swearing, or screaming—at first. His style is to internalize his pressure, comply with what is immediately expected of him, and mull it over until he gets himself so worked up that he lashes out in a manner totally out of character for him— anything from tears to murder. Some of the most vicious crimes committed by people with no criminal records have been accomplished by melancholies under intense pressure. Fortunately, few melancholies react in violence. Most say things of a cutting, hurtful nature for which they are later very repentant. Others ponder the problem and lapse into sulking silence.

Melancholy/cholerics—people who are predominantly melancholy with a secondary temperament of choleric—are the epitomy of workaholics. They react to pressure with intensified work. Their choleric suggests new projects, and their melancholy tries to do everything perfectly. Such individuals are often frustrated by "the pressure of not getting anything done." Others can frustrate them, because they never quite measure up to melancholy perfectionism.

Everyone needs to deal with people by showing concern for them. Melancholies are usually so interested in themselves and their persistent brand of perfectionism that they have little sympathy for and acceptance of other fallible human beings. They would certainly attract more friends if they had more sensitivity. People interested in others never lack for friends.

Everyone needs a diversion—"All work and no play makes Jack a dull boy!"—but melancholies can become so work oriented that they eat, sleep, and think work. Vacations make them feel guilty. The pressure of unfinished work makes it impossible for them to enjoy a simple game of golf. They can turn a relaxing walk through the park into a pressure-filled afternoon.

This inability to relax and learn to cope with the everyday pressures of life will ultimately lead to a breakdown emotionally, mentally, or physically. The melancholy's natural inability to cope with these problems by himself may account for the number of melancholies I have seen come to Christ, dedicate their lives to Him, and learn to walk in the Spirit. When they are truly filled with the Spirit, they experience incredible changes that are immediately apparent to all. However, when they regress spiritually, their friends quickly sense the change. I have great respect for the potential of the person with a predominantly melancholy temperament, but only when he avails himself of the power of God. When he doesn't, his powerlessness is all too evident.

THE PHLEGMATIC TEMPERAMENT

Phlegmatics are calm, easygoing, never-get-upset individuals with such a high boiling point that they almost never become angry. They are without question the easiest people to get along with and are by nature the most likable of all the temperaments.

The phlegmatic derives his name from the Greek word "phlegm," which Hippocrates thought was the cause of his calm, cool, slow, well-balanced temperament. Life for him is a happy, unexcited, pleasant experience in which he avoids as much involvement as possible. He is so calm and unruffled that he never seems agitated, no matter what circumstances surround him. He is the one temperament type which is consistent every time you see him. Beneath his cool, reticent, almost timid personality, Mr. Phlegmatic has a very capable combination of abilities. He feels much more emotion than appears on the surface and has the capacity to appreciate the fine arts and the better things of life.

The phlegmatic does not lack for friends—because he enjoys people and has a natural, dry sense of humor. He is the type of individual who can have a crowd of people "in stitches," yet never cracks a smile. Possessing the unique capability for seeing something humorous in others and the things they do, he maintains a positive approach to life. He has a good retentive mind and is capable of being a fine imitator. One of his great sources of delight is "needling" or poking fun at the other temperament types. For instance, he is annoyed by the aimless, restless enthusiasm of the sanguine and disgusted by the gloomy moods of the melancholy. The former, says Mr. Phlegmatic, must be confronted with his futility, the latter with his morbidity. He takes great delight in throwing ice water on the bubbling plans and ambitions of the choleric.

Phlegmatics tend to be spectators in life and try not to get very involved with the activities of others. In fact, it is usually with great reluctance that they are ever motivated to any form of activity beyond their daily routine. This does not mean, however, that they cannot appreciate the need for action and the predicaments of others. The phlegmatic and choleric may confront the same social injustice, but their response will be entirely different. The crusading spirit of the choleric will cause him to exclaim, "Let's get a committee organized and campaign to do something about this!" The phlegmatic would more likely respond, "These conditions are terrible! Why doesn't someone do something about them?"

Usually kindhearted and sympathetic, a phlegmatic seldom conveys his true feelings. When once aroused to action, however, his capable and efficient qualities become apparent. He will not volunteer for leadership on his own, but when it is forced upon him, he proves to be a very capable leader. He has a conciliating effect on others and is a natural peacemaker.

The world has benefited greatly from the gracious nature of phlegmatics. In their quiet way, they have proved to be fulfillers of the dreams of others. They are masters at anything that requires meticulous patience and daily routine.

Most elementary-school teachers are phlegmatics. Who but a phlegmatic could have the patience necessary to teach a group of first-graders to read? A sanguine would spend the entire class period telling stories to the children. A melancholy would so criticize them that they would be afraid to read aloud. And I can't even imagine a choleric as a first-grade teacher—the students would leap out the windows! The gentle nature of the phlegmatic assures the ideal atmosphere for such learning. This is not only true on the elementary level but in both high school and college, particularly in math, physics, grammar, literature, language classes, and others. It is not uncommon to find phlegmatics as school administrators, librarians, counselors, and college department heads. Phlegmatics seem drawn to the field of educaiton.

Another field that appeals to phlegmatics is engineering. Attracted to planning and calculation, they make good structural engineers, sanitation experts, chemical engineers, draftsmen, mechancial and civil engineers, and statisticians. Most phlegmatics have excellent mechanical aptitude and thus become good mechanics, tool-and-die specialists, craftsmen, carpenters, electricians, plasterers, glassblowers, watch and camera repairmen. . . .

They are well organized, never come to a meeting unprepared or late, tend to work well under pressure, and are extremely dependable. Phlegmatics often stay with one company for their entire working career.

An interesting aspect of their leadership ability is that they almost never volunteer for authoritative responsibilities, which is why I label them "reluctant leaders." Secretly, a phlegmatic may aspire for a promotion, but it would be against his nature to volunteer. Instead, he may patiently wait until more discordant and inept personalities make a mess out of things and then assume the responsibility, only after it is forced upon him. Unfortunately, in many instances phlegmatics wait their lives away and opportunity never knocks—because, although employers appreciate their capabilities, they don't envision them as leaders. Consequently, both the company and the employees lose. Rarely does a phlegmatic either live up to his full capabilities or fail in life.

Because they tend to struggle with the problem of personal insecurity, phlegmatics may take a job with retirement or security benefits in mind. Therefore, civil service, the military, local government, or some other "good security risk" will attract them. Rarely will they launch out on a business venture of their own, although they are eminently qualified to do so. Instead they usually enhance the earning power of someone else and are quite content with a simple life-style.[11]

HOW PHLEGMATICS HANDLE PRESSURE

Phlegmatics detest pressure. In fact, they will do almost anything to avoid it. As we have seen, they do not thrive on controversy, but are peacemakers by nature. Consequently they will always steer around a problem if possible. Unfortunately, ignoring a real problem doesn't make it disappear.

It is easy to diagnose a sanguine's reaction to pressure, for he explodes loudly enough for everyone to see. Phlegmatics are

[11]Ibid., 86–89.

different; as very internal people they do nothing to excess. For this reason you must observe their responses carefully.

Their compulsion to avoid pressure causes many phlegmatics to become gifted procrastinators. This eventually increases their pressures because tasks must be completed sooner or later and final decisions have to be made. Some phlegmatics use the old dodge "we need more information" as an excuse for delaying an unpleasant deed. "Remove the pressure, not the problem" often becomes the phlegmatic way of life.

How well I remember three phlegmatics on a deacon board who appealed for "more time to study the matter" before deciding to expel a leader in the church who had divorced his wife of many years and married another woman. Actually he had made the mistake of marrying the second wife before his divorce was final, and the chapel inadvertently sent his new wedding certificate—signatures, dates, and all—to his home, where Wife No. 1 opened it. The man was a bigamist! Yet the phlegmatics wanted to delay one more month. Why? They rotated off the board before the next meeting.

Problems seldom vanish with time. Rather, they tend to return more robust and intimidating than before. I have found that it is usually best to solve them when they are still small enough to handle.

The phlegmatic under pressure frequently exhibits one exasperating trait: He flees from the pressurized situation. Fathers of rebellious teenagers are likely to sneak out to the garage and putter in their workshop rather than take on their hostile youth. This does nothing for the wife, who laments, "He always leaves the discipline of the children up to me." Phlegmatic wives and mothers often are weak disciplinarians, not because they fail to recognize their children's need for discipline, but because they personally dislike the friction generated by confrontation. Many a phlegmatic employee puts up with years of second-rate treatment at work because he does not relish a confrontation with his boss. "Peace at any price" is not really a solution to anything.

Those who have lived with phlegmatics will acknowledge that they are stubborn. This stubbornness invariably surfaces when someone tries to pressure them into doing something they are unwilling to do. Like a burro, they will dig their feet in, arch their back, and stall. If they fill a place of authority, they can be maddening. Experts on trivia themselves, they can think of more reasons why a building permit or license should not be granted than ever occurred to those who made the laws. Have you ever tried to get something approved by the security-conscious inspectors at city hall? It is nothing short of amazing that the free enterprise system has succeeded in the face of phlegmatic foot-dragging.

Married phlegmatics are quite interesting sexually. A sexuality survey of 3,404 people included a question about temperament. I found that male phlegmatics were less promiscuous before marriage, registered less frequency of sex after marriage, and experienced less satisfaction than their female counterparts. Reflecting on this finding for several years while counseling hundreds of couples, I have come to the following conclusions. Phlegmatics are perfectly normal regarding the place of sexual activity in marriage, and they can be very sexually expressive and loving. They enjoy tenderness, love, and affection, as long as it is not displayed publicly. However, they do not like pressure, conflict, or rejection; consequently they tend to let their partners lead.

I was surprised to discover from my sex survey that a rather high percentage of phlegmatic wives had indicated promiscuity before marriage. Because by nature they like to please others, they would often succumb to the pressure of an aggressive lover's advances. Since opposites usually attract, we should note, phlegmatics often find themselves in the company of more aggressive temperaments. Many of these women indicated that their premarital activity had burdened them with years of guilt.

In the case of the male phlegmatic husband, he has perfectly normal desires but is often reluctant to express them. The pressure of potential rejection tends to inhibit his desires. After marriage the phlegmatic wife usually makes a faithful, responding, and loving partner. Her male counterpart, however, may wait for his wife to show the first interest in lovemaking. Many a choleric or sanguine wife married to a phlegmatic mate has lamented in the counseling room, "I love my husband, he is a wonderful person, but I get so tired of always being the aggressor in our love life." Most women in our Western culture find this humiliating because of the "macho" image we impart to men. Usually I attack this problem through both partners, encouraging the phlegmatic male to be more aggressive and telling the wife that even though he can improve, this is simply his nature. Also, I caution the wives of either melancholies or phlegmatics to read the overture signals very carefully and try not to reject a spouse's offers of love. Otherwise he will become even more passive in this matter.

Phlegmatics are apt to blame other people for their mistakes. Adam must have been phlegmatic, for he started it all by complaining to God, "The woman Thou gavest to be with me, she gave me from the tree, and I ate" (Gen. 3:12, NASB). This seems to be the phlegmatic pattern still. When phlegmatics are confronted with a mistake, a sin, or an error, they will try to cast the blame onto someone else. It's not that they want to be deceitful; they just don't like the pressure of taking the full responsibility for their behavior. Others find this maddening: Parents whose children point the finger at other siblings in the family, or the boss whose otherwise loyal, dependable, and careful employee blames a co-worker under pressure.

The disadvantage of this trait to the phlegmatic himself is that he seldom learns from his behavior. Because blaming others frees him from the immediate pressure, he goes his cheerful way, not admitting that he needs to improve in this regard. As a result, he tends to repeat his mistakes.

Phlegmatic children are great daydreamers. They escape the nasty now by drifting off into a fantasy land. Some have trouble reading, spelling, or learning math because of this. When they grow up, this mental habit will serve as an escape hatch from unpleasant circumstances. No doubt many unhappily married phlegmatics have endured to the end by letting their minds drift to the Land of Oz. But this is not what the Bible means when it says, "Be content with what you have" or "Learn to be content in whatever state you find yourself" (see Heb. 13:5; Phil. 4:11). True contentment comes from God to those who walk with Him. Daydreaming can become a form of unproductive phlegmatic escapism.

SUMMARY OF TEMPERAMENTS

Temperament makes people different. Your involuntary reaction to pressure is a result of your temperament or the intensity of your temperament combination. You are not responsible for your combination of temperaments, for you derived it from your parents at birth. However, now that you know the adverse reaction to pressure of your temperament, you can take steps to improve it. You will be much happier for making the effort. Change will not come easily, and a lifetime of habits cannot easily be broken; but with God's help you can be different.

One of the aspects of life in which to consider change in light of your temperament is your vocation.

TEMPERAMENT AND YOUR VOCATION

You should not become a round peg in a square hole. Many people are frustrated in their jobs, because they don't have the right job. The pay, work conditions, and retirement benefits may be perfect—but the work creates great pressure. Frankly, I can't think of a worse way to exist in a free society than spending forty hours a week doing a job I am not suited for. This may be the greatest single cause of pressure in our country today, because it affects mental attitude. Most people who are temperamentally unsuited for their jobs also have a negative mental attitude.

As a student of temperament and a counselor of more than six thousand people, I have concluded that many people, including Christians who did not seek God's guidance in their early years, are locked into a vocation that is wrong for them. On a scale of 1 to 10, the person whose job ranks 9 or 10 in conjunction with his natural abilities will find satisfaction in his work. If the job rates a 4 or 5, he will feel unnecessary pressure.

During the past fifteen years I have developed a temperament test that can be completed in thirty to forty minutes. In testing nearly twenty thousand people, we have found it to be more than 90 percent accurate, which is excellent in comparison with secular-market tests. The final, personalized report includes a fifteen-page description of a person's predominant and secondary temperaments and suggests fifty different vocations for which a person is suited. There are several other features, such as how to overcome your ten greatest weaknesses and how to diagnose your major spiritual gifts. If you are uncertain about your vocation and your natural qualifications, the test will prove helpful. Undue vocational pressure is unnecessary.

I agree with Bill Gothard's concept that what you enjoy doing most is usually the will of God for your life. If you are not happy with your occupation, you not only need to take the temperament test, but should sincerely seek God's guidance in a special way.

I have advised many men and women to begin such a vocational quest with two prayers.

1. Offer a prayer of confession regarding all known sin. The psalmist said, "If I regard iniquity in my heart, the Lord will not hear" (Ps. 66:18).

2. Once your heart is free of sin, submit yourself totally and unconditionally to God (see Rom. 6:11–13). Your will is usually the greatest hindrance to finding the will of God, for it often makes you deaf to His leading. I have found through many years that His way is *always* best. In fact, some day I may write a book on "The Stops of the Lord"—that is, God's negative response to certain insistent requests. Today I look back and say, "Thank you, Lord!"

By faith accept the fact that God is alive, He loves you, and He has a plan for your life. He is the potter; you are the clay (Isa. 64:8). This helps you to know that God's will is for your *good*. I have refused to join the "Christian Sadist Cult" that insinuates that one is out of God's will if he enjoys what he is doing.

Here is a visual practice that I have found helpful: Conceptualize your body (while praying) lying on an altar of sacrifice (Rom. 12:1). Tell God you are totally His, every member of your body from the top of your head to the soles of your feet. Then get up and anticipate God's leading. When you find a door of opportunity, enter prayerfully, seeking His "peace" (see Col. 3:15) and testing it to make sure it does not violate any known Scripture (Col. 3:16–17). Move ahead by faith and do the best job you can; when you complete that responsibility, He will open another door. Remember Jesus' promise in Revelation 3:7–8,

> "And to the angel of the church in Philadelphia write: He who is holy, who is true, who has the key of David, *who opens and no one will shut,* and *who shuts and no one opens,* says this: 'I know your deeds. Behold, *I have put before you an open door which no one can shut,* because you have a little power, and have kept My word, and have not denied My name'" (NASB).

Your Savior is also the God of the open door. Let Him open the door to your ultimate opportunity, and when He does, go in. Never limit Him by the unbelief of not taking advantage of His obvious leadings.

CHAPTER 8

Pressure—The Good Motivator

"Man shall earn his bread by the sweat of his face" (Gen. 3:19).

"He that doesn't work shouldn't eat" (2 Thess. 3:10).

Do you know what is far worse than intense pressure? Never having anything to do. Work is not a duty; it is a mental, physical, emotional, and spiritual necessity. Most people have the wrong idea about work. God has given it to us as an instrument for good. Even Adam and Eve had responsibilities to fulfill in the Garden of Eden *before* the Fall.

Few things are more satisfying and fulfilling in life than a good job well done, whether raising a family, building a house, restoring an old car, or leading a person to Christ. The degree of fulfillment depends on the value a person places on the work or experience. I am confident there is no lasting happiness and satisfaction in life without diligence and strenuous effort.

Hard work never hurt anyone, and the right kind of activity performed with the proper attitude is extremely beneficial. My father was a machine repairman at the Ford auto plant in Dearborn, Michigan. He was responsible for keeping forty-four machines running at primary efficiency. He loved his work. Whenever frustrated operators came to him complaining about a machinery malfunction, a new light gleamed in his eye as he channeled all his energies into solving the problem. He would work around the clock, even through mealtimes, to get the machine operating again. When he came home after such a day, he had a spring in his step and a whistle on his lips. He was tired, but not fatigued. His worst days were those when all his machines operated smoothly, leaving him with nothing to do. On such occasions the song in his heart faded and he returned home exhausted.

Fatigue is mental exhaustion. Some people wake up in the morning fatigued, because they have no meaningful work to perform. It is a matter of motivation. Tiredness is physical exhaustion that usually responds to rest, a good meal (to raise the blood-sugar level), or some form of diversion. Interestingly, the diversion is usually another form of work.

I must be a source of frustration to my insurance agent, because he has been totally unsuccessful in getting me to think intelligently about a retirement policy. Somehow the thought of not having meaningful work to do does not arouse me. When I go on vacation, I take a box of books along. The most memorable trip Beverly and I ever took was a month-long visit to Europe. Besides enjoying sightseeing and travel, I read seventeen books. Consequently I came home refreshed.

We have to repudiate the idea that work is drudgery or might be harmful. I have noticed that retirement is dangerous for some people. Have you observed how rapidly many people age or deteriorate when they retire? They simply have not infused meaningful work into their retirement. Benjamin Franklin rightly said, "There is nothing wrong with retirement as long as one doesn't allow it to interfere with his work."

One philosopher noted that man is a working creature and that the chief characteristic of mankind is not his wisdom but his work. I am inclined to believe that work and wisdom go together. "Leisure" does not mean the cessation of labor. A "man of leisure" is someone who enjoys his present activity. I have written many books just because I enjoy writing. Reports from my readers that the books have met a need only enhances the enjoyment.

PRESSURE AND MOTIVATION

Work produces pressure, but pressure engenders motivation. You have probably noticed this on a Saturday morning when you have nothing to do. On weekdays you may awaken at six o'clock, but on Saturday, if your wife or children are quiet, you can sleep till eight or nine. To change that format, try making a list just before you go to bed Friday night, of what you want to accomplish Saturday.

It isn't only work that fires you, but the proper motivation that results from the right mental attitude to the pressure of the task at hand. If you go to bed so depressed after making a list of Saturday duties that you awaken fatigued, schedule a golfing date or a shopping spree for Saturday morning. Mental attitude toward pressure usually makes the difference between stress and distress.

A number of books have been written on the subject of stress in recent years. All authorities recognize both positive and negative stress. Hans Selye, the pioneer authority in the field, defines stress as "the consequence of demand made upon the body." The definition is neutral, for the stress can be either bad or good. If two people are performing exactly the same task, it may produce positive stress and motivation in one, and negative stress—distress—in the other. I do not share my father's enjoyment at the challenge of activating a broken machine. The same tasks that provided positive stress for him offers frustration and negative stress to me.

Negative pressure or positive pressure with a negative mental attitude will inevitably produce negative motivation. Positive pressure or even negative pressure with a positive mental attitude produces positive motivation. Study the chart on the next page.

I have seen all kinds of pressure transformed into positive motivation from horribly negative motivation merely by a

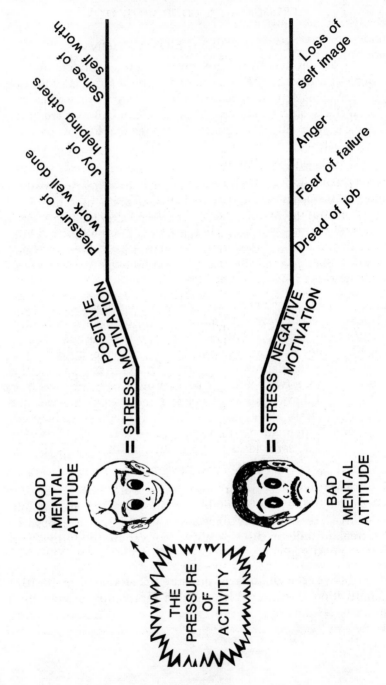

change of mental attitude. For instance, for those who live under the pressure of an unhappy marriage and biblically do not approve of divorce, the only recourse is to summon the grace and power of God to produce a change of mental attitude. Only with a positive attitude will the faithful partner be able to endure the strain.

Many times the pressures of life are enlarged out of proportion by a faulty mental attitude. Anyone who dwells on criticism or indulges in selfish or self-centered thinking will compound his pressures. The woman confined to the home with three preschool children, for instance, will feel intense pressure unless she maintains a positive mental attitude.

Consider the man who despises his job. His sense of pressure will persist unless he changes his mental attitude. One man griped to me, "I feel trapped. I hate my job but I have to work." I challenged him to stop finding fault with his job and to discover some aspects of it he liked. He couldn't. Then one day he came to the counseling session in a much more positive mood. Why? He had met a man of his age and skill level who was jobless. For the first time he felt grateful for his job, and then the pressures eased. He still plodded through the same undesirable work activities, but he experienced less pressure.

I know of nothing that will change a person's mental attitude faster than the practice of thanksgiving. Even as I write, I am forcing myself to practice what I preach. We are in San Jose, California, for banquet 107 to promote our TV program and we are at least two thousand "faith partners" away from breaking even financially. I am turning down many invitations to air our program because Bev and I simply cannot afford to subsidize the ministry any more than we are at present. We are staying in an old hotel where the air conditioning doesn't work and the air is stifling; all kinds of blunders have made this less than a successful banquet. To be honest, it is a struggle to think positively. Some people would blame Satan for the kind of thoughts that come to my mind; I blame my choleric/sanguine temperament and my miserable disposition. Victory over my emotional state will not come simply by positive thinking, for I am too much of a realist to rejoice over incompetence. Instead, I find victory in thanking God for an abundance of positive things:

Life, health, His faithfulness, and what He means to me. Maintaining a positive mental attitude greatly reduces pressure. The pressure doesn't disappear, but at least thanksgiving whittles it down to size so I can live with it.

A good slogan to follow is "Use your pressure before it uses you." The next chapter will show you how to do it.

We have already considered three dangers that intensify pressure:

1. The loss of control over one's circumstances
2. The duration of pressure beyond normal limits
3. The absence of light at the end of the tunnel

Another is frustration. According to Dr. Selye,

> Blocking the fulfillment of man's natural drives causes as much distress as the forced prolongation and intensification of any activity beyond the desired level. Ignoring this rule leads to frustration, fatigue, and exhaustion which can progress to a mental or physical breakdown.[1]

No one likes to have his plans, efforts, or dreams nullified. But frustration is a part of life. That is, everyone sooner or later encounters resistance or failure. Even the most determined person must eventually take no for an answer. The motto previously given was: "Never take no for an answer until you hear it eight or nine times." This doesn't always work, and in time, the pressure of frustration may increase; but at least it keeps you from wondering later on what could have been done had you tried just one more time. I am convinced that frustration can cause pressure, but this same pressure may be salutary if it does not persevere beyond reasonable bounds.

USE PRESSURE AS A MOTIVATER

Most people have the wrong attitude toward pressure, considering it exclusively harmful. By now you must recognize that is not always true. Most of our accomplishments in life are achieved because of pressure. Consider marriage, for instance. How many people marry *after* they have ridden out the third wave of libido? The first wave hits between ages 16 and 21, which is when most people marry. The next rolls shoreward

---

[1]Selye, *Stress Without Distress.*

around ages 23–25. Then the third wave breaks at 27–30. Someone has facetiously observed, "If you can ride out the first three waves of libido, you have enough sense to get married." That is probably only a half-truth, for at this stage in life one's motivation is so low that he may pass up some good opportunities. In fact, too many people in our culture practice promiscuity during their twenties and remain single late into life. I'm not convinced this is advantageous for either society or these individuals. Sexual pressure is an instrument of God to perpetuate the family, life, and love. We ignore it at our peril.

When pressures arise that are normal and good, we need to use them for our benefit. I have a son who didn't want to attend college after finishing high school. One summer on a construction crew produced enough pressure to propel him back to the books. As the pastor of a growing church, I had more than my share of work. Yet I took the time to write books. I used the trick of pressuring myself by making a time commitment that really motivated me. I had noticed, for instance, that when I announced in church that one month hence I would inaugurate a series of messages and provide printed copies each week, attendance increased 25–30 percent. Keeping that schedule involved intense pressure, but it motivated me to do the research and writing, and in turn I pressured others to do the typing, editing, printing, and collating. Sometimes the ink was still wet, but we managed to distribute the materials on time. Admittedly my family enjoyed me more when I was not in the middle of a series, but unless I committed myself to the pressure of a deadline, there was no finished product.

By contrast, I encounter ministers all over the country who tell me that they want to write books. Quite typically this pastor has just finished a significant series of sermons or biblical studies that deserve to be in print. Yet I have never known such a minister to get the work into publishable form unless the chapters are ghost-written from tapes. Why not? Because, when the pressure to complete the series has subsided, the minister is faced with new pressure to study for the next series. Whenever two pressures come into conflict, the stronger will win. The pressure to prepare next Sunday's sermon will always take precedence over writing down last month's series.

ANOTHER GOOD USE OF PRESSURE

One technique I have used through the years forces me to finish writing a book on schedule: Keen anticipation of the next book. For some reason I usually tire of the writing about three-fourths of the way through the manuscript, and excitement about the next project makes me impatient to move ahead. But energetic work on the new book will drain all my psychic energy, preventing completion of the book I am working on. Eventually I learned that if I refuse to permit myself to do preparatory reading or serious writing on the second book until I finish the first, I have added motivation to meet my obligations.

People who complete tasks well in life don't necessarily work harder than others; they simply force themselves to finish one job before tackling another. I visited an artist's studio and found a half-dozen unfinished paintings lying around. When the painter became hungry enough—a form of pressure—he finished and sold one or more of his works.

I know very few "self-starting" people. Most of us need a degree of pressure, which is actually a form of commitment—that is, self-commitment to a project with sufficient guidelines and deadlines to motivate us to complete the appointed task. Those who are unwilling to assume this much pressure usually end up accomplishing little in life. They may be creative, talented, or capable, but they just don't use the power of self-inflicted pressure through commitment to motivate them to reach their potential.

Don't be afraid of pressure, particularly in short-term, controlled doses. Use it for self-motivation. This is especially important to phlegmatics. As we saw in chapter 7, each temperament reacts differently to pressure. Phlegmatics tend to ignore, avoid, or endure it. They will avoid it if at all possible, but for them this is a mistake. One of the best lessons for a phlegmatic to learn from the temperament theory is that he is not by nature internally motivated. For this reason he should accept external pressure through commitment. Fortunately he is usually very dependable, so once he makes such a commitment, he will predictably follow through. The phlegmatic who does not utilize external pressure to motivate him rarely achieves his potential.

Although the other temperaments do not need external pressure to motivate them, to one degree or another we can all use it for motivation—in controlled doses.

All this is said to help you realize that pressure may be your friend rather than your enemy. Watch for the danger signs already mentioned: Don't let pressure get out of control or last too long, and try to look for the light at the end of the tunnel. As long as you can do that, your pressure can be an activator rather than destructive.

Remember, God has designed the human body with an amazing ability to adjust to the complexities of life. When you are exposed to communicable diseases, your natural immunity system leaps into action to protect you. If you lose an eye or ear, scientists tell us, the remaining organs sharpen and intensify as if to compensate for the loss. So it is with your system's ability to cope with normal pressure.

A reasonable amount of short-term pressure never killed anyone. We may think it will harm us as we endure a pressurized situation, but it won't. The fear that pressure will adversely affect us only serves to compound it. Again, remember amid pressure that, according to 1 Corinthians 10:13, it will not destroy you, for God will offer a way of escape. I find it helpful to keep reminding myself, "Things aren't really out of control; they only seem that way."

We all envision that a summer vacation will be full of relaxation and devoid of pressure. I have never found this to be the case. I can remember the time at Lake Powell in Utah when I sheered off the drive end of our outboard motor by hitting a rock just beneath the surface of the water. It surely disrupted our plans for water-skiing and created family pressure. We cannot avoid pressure, so we might as well learn to use it productively.

Pressure, then, can be healthful and motivating if it doesn't last too long, doesn't get out of control, and is faced with the right mental attitude. Trying to avoid it altogether will guarantee failure. Pressure produces stress, stress generates energy (ACTH), and energy enriches your life.

The following chart will further illustrate what I have explained:

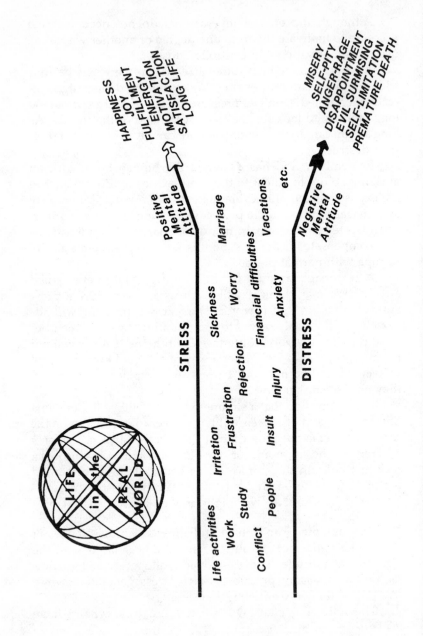

CHAPTER 9

How to Maintain
a Good Mental Attitude

The key to managing pressure is to maintain a good mental attitude. I have stated this about ten times so far, in different ways, because it is so important.

More significant than circumstances, people, financial or physical conditions, or any other single factor in managing pressure is the state of your mental attitude. Everything may seem to be working perfectly, but a poor attitude can negate it all. Conversely, although pressures can be great—sufficient to sink normal people—one can still rise above it all by maintaining a proper mental attitude.

People from all stations of life have come to my counseling room, exhibiting both good and bad mental attitudes and convincing me that it is not how you look, but how you *think* you look that is important. It is not how much money you have, but how much money *means* to you that makes the difference. Mental attitude is the most important factor in handling pressure. This is why God said, "As a man thinketh in his heart, so is he" (Prov. 23:7). He amplified this in Mark 7:21–23:

> For from within, out of men's hearts, come evil thoughts,
> sexual immorality, theft, murder, adultery, greed, malice, deceit,
> lewdness, envy, slander, arrogance and folly. All these evils come
> from inside and make a man "unclean" (NIV).

Because proper mental attitude is so important, we will exam-

143

ine the essential steps in maintaining it. Only then will we be ready to learn how to control pressure.

1. KNOW WHO YOU ARE

More than 13 million young people are said to be attending college in this country, and 85 percent of them take sophomore psychology in the hope that they will discover who they are. Some even admit that the identity crisis is one of the greatest problems on the college campus today. Why? Because it is the major problem in life.

Although most young people think psychologists can help them find themselves, this has proved to be a vain hope, because many psychologists took up that study in the first place to find *their* identity. They have discovered psychology to be a field of study that raises many questions and offers few answers. Unfortunately it is unable to solve the identity question.

For centuries man has attempted to discover who he is. Philosophers and sages from every culture have tried to provide answers, but all searched in vain unless they sought the truth from the Creator, who alone has a valid answer. Actually four questions must be dealt with together in discovering identity. They are basic, but not impossible to answer if we take the Word of God at face value. Most Sunday school children know the answers before they enter the fifth grade: *Who am I? Where did I come from? Why am I here? Where am I going?*

This subject is crucial. I have already dealt with it in two previous books, but because it is so essential to formulating a good mental attitude, it is important to discuss briefly here.

WHO ARE YOU?

You are a child of God, or can be. John 1:12–13 states, "Yet to all who receive Him, to those who believed in His name, He gave the right to become children of God—children born not of natural descent, nor of human decision or a husband's will, but born of God."

Once you have received Jesus Christ by faith, you are "a child of God," making you the most important individual in the universe. You do not have to see yourself as a biological accident, the result of the long processes of evolution planned by no one and accountable to no one, as secular educators contend. You are not just another animal. You are a special creature of God. To be also "a child of God" by faith in Jesus Christ is even better.

It is impossible to overestimate the importance of that fact, for it influences—or should influence—every thought that enters your mind and everything you do. When you confront the difficulties and pressures of life as a child of God, you are never alone. You face them with the realistic confidence that your heavenly Father, the omnipotent God of all creation, is interested in you, His child.

WHERE DID YOU COME FROM?

I have already alluded to the answer to this question: You were created by a loving, almighty God. In a day when many intellectuals heavily steeped in the atheistic thoughts of secular humanism are using our public schools to destroy such innate beliefs in the minds of our children, you need to remind yourself periodically what God's Word says about your origin.

> In the beginning was the Word, and the Word was with God, and the Word was God. He was with God in the beginning. Through him all things were made; without him nothing was made that has been made (John 1:1–3, NIV).

> He is the image of the invisible God, the first-born of all creation. For by him all things were created: things in heaven and on earth, visible and invisible, whether thrones or powers or rulers or authorities; all things were created by him and for him. He is before all things, and in him all things hold together (Col. 1:15–17, NIV).

WHY AM I HERE?

The belief that man is an evolutionary accident, the highest form of primate, offers no challenging purpose for living. This should never be the lot of a "child of God."

> For we are God's workmanship, created in Christ Jesus to do good works, which God prepared in advance for us to do (Eph. 2:10, NIV).

The apostle Paul—everyone's choice as the outstanding Christian of all time—never lost sight of who he was and why he was here. Repeatedly he referred to himself as "the bondservant of Jesus Christ." From the time of his salvation—when he prayed, "Lord, what will you have me to do?" (see Acts 22:10)—to his swan song to Timothy—"I have fought the good fight, I have finished my course, I have kept the faith" (2 Tim. 4:7)—Paul affirmed that he was on this earth to serve his Lord. Within these lifetime parameters he lived and taught the principle, "Therefore, we are ambassadors for Christ . . ." (2 Cor. 5:20).

During his earthly ministry Paul faced incredible pressure.

> Rather, as servants of God we commend ourselves in every way: in great endurance; in troubles, hardships and distresses; in beatings, imprisonments and riots; in hard work, sleepless nights and hunger; in purity, understanding, patience and kindness; in the Holy Spirit and in sincere love; in truthful speech and in the power of God; with weapons of righteousness in the right hand and in the left; through glory and dishonor, bad report and good report; genuine, yet regarded as imposters; known, yet regarded as unknown; dying, and yet we live on; beaten, and yet not killed; sorrowful, yet always rejoicing; poor, yet making many rich; having nothing, and yet possessing everything (2 Cor. 6:4–17, NIV).

Through it all Paul never lost sight of who he was, where he came from, or why he was here. That is essential to maintaining a good mental attitude.

WHERE AM I GOING?

Intellectuals educated in secular humanism's atheistic theories, as well as their millions of victims, stumble through life still not knowing why they are here and where they are going. American affluence seems to compound their futility. In poor countries people without faith are at least forced to work diligently just to sustain life. In our country hard work is an option, leisure the goal. This gives the empty theories of humanism a chance to expose their futile ways. Those who cannot endure the pressure of a purposeless existence resort to marijuana, strong drink, sex, pornography, lavish entertainment, and a host of other balms to soothe their troubled minds. Man innately must have a reason to live; otherwise he concludes, like the philosopher of Ecclesiastes, "All is vanity."

Such an empty way of life should never grip the Christian.

He is here for a purpose that is greater than himself. The object of his existence is to serve God. The most fulfilled, contented, and happy people I know are toiling for Jesus Christ with all their heart, mind, and soul.

One of the privileges of being in the ministry for thirty years and traveling as much as I do—to more than 150 cities in one year—is that I can meet some of the finest servants in our Lord's army. Almost universally they disregard traditional work schedules—some work 60–80 hours a week. They usually skip all or half of their vacations, rarely think of retiring, and when questioned are found to be positive, forward-thinking people. They eagerly anticipate the life *after* this one. They are following in the footsteps of Moses.

> He regarded disgrace for the sake of Christ as of greater value than the treasures of Egypt, because he was looking ahead to his reward (Heb. 11:26, NIV).

Paul, the most motivated of all Christians on record, left us the secret of his drive.

> Now there is in store for me the crown of righteousness, which the Lord, the righteous Judge, will award to me on that day—and not only to me, but also to all who have longed for his appearing (2 Tim. 4:8, NIV).

Anytime a Christian fails to maintain a positive mental attitude, it is because he has lost sight of who and whose he is. If you have a problem in this regard, concentrate on the biblical answer to these questions rather than your feelings; gradually you will begin to develop a better mental attitude. You should at least take great courage in knowing that God made you for a purpose and has a plan for your future. If that isn't enough, consider the supreme evidence of God's love and concern for you in giving His only begotten Son for your forgiveness, salvation, and eternal life.

2. ACCEPT YOURSELF AS GOD MADE YOU

I have noted that anyone with a bad mental attitude (which invariably surfaces under pressure) has a problem with self-acceptance. We hear much talk about this problem today, because it is both very important and very widespread. I have come to the conclusion that everyone starts out in life with an inferiority complex. We are all little people in a big world, feeling unskilled and inept while everyone else is capable. As we mature and learn certain skills, the feeling should recede. Unfortunately, some people reject themselves all the way to the grave.

In my book *How to Win Over Depression,* I devote an entire chapter to self-acceptance and how to attain it. Therefore I will offer only some essential concepts here.

Your ability to accept yourself, your looks, your talents, your family, your environment, and your future will influence your relationship to God, people, and everything you do in life. Thus it is imperative that you come to grips with who and what you are. Naturally this is easier for Christians once they accept themselves as special objects of God's love and creative design; but it is not automatic.

Most people have their greatest difficulties with their looks and talents. This is unfortunate, because we (including these two qualities) were designed by God's creative manipulation of the genes at the time of conception. Therefore you should thank God for the way He made you. As the prophet sagely said in Isaiah 45:9, "Woe to him who quarrels with his Maker, to him who is but a potsherd among the potsherds on the ground. Does the clay say to the potter, 'What are you making?' Does your work say, 'He has no hands'?" (NIV).

I have shared the following therapeutic technique with many who reject themselves. Frankly examine what you don't like or tend to resent about yourself, and thank God specifically by faith for that. Then each time it comes to mind, remember to verbalize your thanksgiving. Most of us have to do this by faith, which is permissible. Just do it!

Perhaps a personal illustration will clarify the concept. As a young man I resented that God made me only five-foot-seven. Since I am well-cordinated, did well at most sports except basketball, and have the drive of a larger person, I made the air force football team as a middle linebacker on the "thied string." I could stop running plays, but smart quarterbacks could easily lob passes over my head.

Later in life I realized that my attitude was affecting my

relationship to God. There was an undercurrent of resentfulness that did not result in a spirit of thanksgiving. While following my own therapy outline and trying to remember to thank God for being the ideal height (for me), I boarded a plane in Boston bound for Los Angeles. The man behind me was extremely restless—twisting, jerking, and gyrating in his seat. About the time I decided to speak to him, I turned and found that he was the seven-foot-two center for the Boston Celtics basketball team. That was the first time I realized how comfortably a five-seven frame fits into airplane seats—and I have spent a major part of my life on airplanes. God doesn't make mistakes. We just sometimes think He does.

"Beauty is in the eye of the beholder," the saying reminds us. You are as beautiful or handsome as you think you are. Two of the most beautiful women I ever counseled came to see me because they considered themselves homely.

Plastic surgery is a booming business, according to a recent *U.S. News & World Report*. However, surgeons are not magicians. If the patient has a problem with self-image before the surgery, it will perpetuate itself afterward. A survey taken in Hollywood among twelve "beautiful people" asked, "If you had the power to change anything about your facial appearance, what would it be?" The least number was *eight items*. If twelve of Hollywood's best "lookers" would change eight or more of their facial characteristics, don't be surprised if you sometimes wish you could modify your features.

The same can be said for skills. We would all choose a different set of abilities if we could. Fortunately for us, that has been decided by God. We can preserve our looks and upgrade our skills, but we can never change the basic ingredients.

We can, however, accept ourselves as we are: Creatures of God. If we don't, it really doesn't matter how good-looking or talented we may be; our gripy, discontented attitude will negate our effectiveness and potential.

One verse of Scripture has helped millions of people: "He who did not spare His own Son, but gave Him up for us all—how will He not also, along with Him, graciously give us all things?" (Rom. 8:32, NIV). You are the special object of God's love. Jesus Christ's death on the cross proves that. Therefore, as

He promised, "No good thing does he withhold from those whose walk is blameless" (Ps. 84:11, NIV).

3. DEVELOP A THANKSGIVING ATTITUDE

One of the most important truths I have discovered since becoming a Christian is the need to maintain a thanksgiving attitude—about everything.

There are only two kinds of people: Gripers and Thankers (some identify them as Groaners and Praisers). Gripers are never happy; Thankers always are. You have the capacity to be either, but if you allow the Spirit of God to control your mind, you will be a Thanker.

A very specific command in the Bible—to "be filled with the Spirit" (or, controlled by the Spirit)—is found in Ephesians 5:18. It is pointed out that the second result of His "filling" or "control" will be a thanksgiving attitude—"always giving thanks to God the Father for everything, in the name of our Lord Jesus Christ" (Eph. 5:20, NIV).

In Psalm 1:1, God warns us against sitting around with Gripers. Throughout the Old Testament God denounces and condemns Gripers (Israel in the wilderness, Moses, Elijah, Jeremiah, and others).

By contrast, in both the Old and New Testaments we read hundreds of challenges to thanksgiving. First Thessalonians 5:18 makes it clear that anything else is to be out of the will of God: "Give thanks in all circumstances, for this is God's will for you in Christ Jesus" (NIV).

I am convinced that one cannot be lastingly happy or learn how to control pressure unless he develops the mental habit of thanksgiving. And that is not easy. Personally I have to work on it constantly. After all these years of teaching, writing and trying to practice a thanksgiving mental attitude, one would think it becomes automatic. Not so! I look on the development of a habitual thanksgiving mental attitude as if it were a large boulder which I consciously push uphill everyday. If I unconsciously forget thanksgiving, the stone rolls back down the hill a few yards, so I must start pushing again. It gets easier only as I walk in the Spirit and try to be grateful by thanking God for His goodness in the things I understand, and by thanking Him by faith for what He is going to do in the things I do not understand. Thanksgiving is imperative; otherwise you will drift into griping, which will destroy your positive mental attitude and increase your pressure.

Thanksgiving living—developing a thanksgiving mental attitude—is not only "the will of God" for your life, but the secret to developing a positive mental attitude, which in turn is the key to controlling pressure. Admittedly, thanksgiving is not an easy habit or way of life to develop, but it is absolutely essential.

Some temperaments find thanksgiving to be easier than others, but I do not read in Scripture that God commands only sanguines and phlegmatics, "In everything give thanks." This is a universal command to us all, and it must be obeyed. Otherwise our life's pressures will control us instead of our controlling them.

Anyone who desires to work seriously on developing a thanksgiving mental attitude should do the following:

• Do a daily Bible study on all the verses related to thanksgiving. Write down your findings.

• Memorize one thanksgiving verse per week, starting with 1 Thessalonians 5:18 and Philippians 4:6–7.

• Read Philippians through daily for thirty days.

• Make a list of ten characteristics about your spouse (if married) or closest relative or friend (if single), giving thanks for each one daily for three months.

• Make a list of ten other items for which you are grateful, thanking God for them daily.

• Do not permit your mind to think negatively, critically, or ungratefully—and never repeat such thoughts verbally. If you do, repent as soon as you realize what you have done, confess it as sin, and replace the thought with something for which you are truly grateful. Then quote one of the thanksgiving verses you have been memorizing.

When I am in a grouchy mood, I have found that rehearsing aloud the promises of God and the blessings for which I should give thanks is helpful. Hearing the sound of my own voice quoting the Scriptures is reassuring.

Even as I wrote this chapter, I found the whole procedure

highly beneficial. After months of traveling, I returned to a building project that was behind schedule and a quiet mountain hideaway (where I was to finish this book) that resembled the Los Angeles freeway at rush hour. Plan B offered no improvement, so Beverly and I returned home, where the temperature was 104 degrees, the kitchen table was gone, and I was forced to write on a wobbly card table. Only the therapy of thanksgiving could give respite at such a moment.

Without consciously practicing thanksgiving, you will never develop a lasting positive mental attitude.

4. LEARN TO BE CONTENT WHERE YOU ARE

"But godliness with contentment is great gain" (1 Tim. 6:6, NIV).

"Keep your lives free from the love of money and be content with what you have, because God has said, 'Never will I leave you; never will I forsake you'" (Heb. 13:5, NIV).

"I am not saying this because I am in need, for I have learned to be content whatever the circumstances. I know what it is to be in need, and I know what it is to have plenty. I have learned the secret of being content in any and every situation, whether well fed or hungry, whether living in plenty or in want. I can do everything through Him who gives me strength" (Phil. 4:11–13, NIV).

The man who generalized contentment "whatever the circumstances" and "in every situation" was the church's most celebrated jailbird. Paul had been imprisoned many times for faithfully preaching the Gospel. Instead of griping and groaning, he had "learned to be content." How? By practicing the art of praise in a situation that would naturally breed complaints. Our modern jails are luxurious palaces by comparison with the Mamertine prison in Rome, where Paul was incarcerated. I have seen it—or one like it—and it was dreadful. Lacking bars, lights, or creature comforts, it was a cold, damp cave with one opening at the top through which the prisoner was lowered. After he was there, only his sparse food supply passed through that opening. Yet he had learned to be content.

Your prison may be an overcrowded apartment with more children than bedrooms, an office without windows, a car that barely runs, or a job well beneath your ability and income needs. It may be an unhappy marriage or overly possessive parents. Whatever the privation or predicament, have you *learned* to be content? If not, you can never gain contentment by moving to a bigger apartment, getting a new job, or leaving your partner. Most people want to change their circumstances as a means to achieving peace. To the contrary, satisfaction is learned by developing a thanksgiving attitude where you are. Your present circumstances may not be Shangri-la, but they *are* your training ground. Since God wants to teach you contentment, learn your lesson as quickly as possible so He can speed you on to where He wants you to be. I am inclined to believe that many Christians spend their lives in the prison of discontent because they refused to learn the lesson of satisfaction where they are.

Remaining cheerfully serene in the face of unpleasant circumstances is possible only through developing the art of "thanksgiving living." Thanking God for your present address in life is the first giant step toward learning contentment.

MY FAVORITE BIBLE CHARACTER

King David was known as "the man after God's own heart," King Solomon as "the wisest man who ever lived," Jeremiah as "the weeping prophet," Moses as "the law giver" and "the meekest man in the Bible," Samson as "the strongest man in the Old Testament," and John the Baptist as "the greatest man born of woman." But my favorite Bible character is Caleb, one of the two faithful spies (with Joshua) who brought back a positive report of the Promised Land filled with milk and honey.

In the darkest hours of our television ministry, when we were running a $31,000-a-month deficit, I had trouble sleeping. I found it very helpful to get up at 3 A.M. (tossing and turning only served to keep my wife awake anyway) and read the Bible. One morning I was fighting depression with everything I had. My natural thought lamented, "Who needs this? I've never worked harder in my life, but I've been repeatedly deceived, betrayed, and frustrated. I'm trying to help millions of people with biblical principles, and although everyone seems to favor a high-quality TV product that does not beg for money on television, only a small percentage of Christians are willing to join us in this step of faith to make it possible." These represented only a few of the self-pitying thoughts that were bringing on my depression. Then I read Numbers 13–15 and Joshua 14–15.

That morning last fall was not the first time I had studied Caleb's life, for I had often read Numbers 14:24: "But My servant Caleb, because *he has had a different spirit and has followed Me fully*, I will bring into the land which he entered, and his descendants shall take possession of it" (NASB). Whenever I read that, I pray, "Oh God, give me that kind of spirit—the other spirit that set Caleb apart from all the rest. I too want to follow you *fully*, obedient to all you teach and confident that you will keep Your Word."

Every Christian can pray this prayer. We don't all have the same pressures, but we all face pressure. Each of us needs that "other spirit" of faith, a dimension that pushes us on to accomplish the will of God in the face of impossible circumstances —or learn contentment while living in the midst of intolerable circumstances. Contentment makes the unbearable bearable.

Caleb has been a blessing, because I have had to learn contentment while doing something I absolutely detest. I dislike chicken and I dislike certain aspects of fund-raising. Yet at 139 of the first 145 banquets held during the year when we were starting our TV ministry, we served chicken. Another hundred or more banquets were envisioned, with the same prospect of eating chicken and the same personal pressures of fund-raising.

"Why do you pursue that route if you dislike it so?" you may ask. Because television is the most powerful vehicle to reach the minds of millions of people in the shortest period of time. People watch TV rather than go to church, attend sporting events, or read books. A recent survey disclosed that more than 22 million people in this country watch religious programs regularly, rating them their third-favorite type of program (behind news and sports). It is noteworthy in the survey that 10 percent of those who watch Christian programs regularly are unsaved. My wife and I sincerely believe that God has led us to use this electronic medium to reach the millions of hurting families in this country with His biblical principles for family living. There are only four ways to finance any kind of television programming: (1) Persuade advertisers to sponsor the shows, the way secular humanist "entertainment" is sponsored; (2) Persuade foundations to give grants to finance programming, as liberal humanists do for public broadcasting; (3) Appeal on the air for people to send donations, and (4) Travel across the country, holding banquets and inviting people to become "faith partners" who send monthly contributions.

Somehow Christian manufacturers, businessmen, and foundations have not yet seen the wisdom of using the free enterprise system to advance the kingdom of God the way the humanists have used it to undermine the religious and traditional moral values of our nation. One hopes some of these companies will one day recognize the need to sponsor programs with their advertising dollars. With 69 million "born-again" adults in our population (according to the Gallup Poll), it is just a matter of time until some marketing organization realizes that it could be highly profitable to aim some advertising at that market. Until that happens, it will be necessary for us to hold an endless series of fund-raising banquets to finance the television ministry.

In the meantime, I have learned contentment while doing something I do not particularly enjoy—the same lesson Caleb learned during his forty years in the wilderness. Have you ever spent time in the desert? We used to attend motorcycle campouts in the Mojave Desert. After four days I was ready for home and a hot shower! Yet Caleb spent forty years in the wilderness of Sinai as punishment for *someone else's* sin. Though he had done no wrong, he "followed the Lord fully." He even interrupted the faithless spies in their evil report.

> Then Caleb quieted the people before Moses, and said, "We should by all means go up and take possession of it, for we shall surely overcome it" (Num. 13:30, NASB).
>
> And Joshua the son of Nun and Caleb the son of Jephunneh, of those who had spied out the land, tore their clothes; and they spoke to all the congregation of the sons of Israel, saying, "The land which we passed through to spy out is an exceedingly good land. If the LORD is pleased with us, then He will bring us into this land, and give it to us—a land which flows with milk and honey.

Only do not rebel against the LORD; and do not fear the people of the land, for they shall be our prey. Their protection has been removed from them, and the LORD is with us; do not fear them" (Num. 14:6–9, NASB).

Yet the people rejected this counsel and chose to believe the ten faithless spies. God sentenced those unbelieving adults to die in the wilderness for their unbelief. Thus the families of Joshua and Caleb were forced to plod for forty years through the wilderness.

Most Christians would have spent that time griping, criticizing their companions' unbelief, and complaining about the transient living conditions. Not Caleb. He married, raised children, and must have spent considerable time as a pallbearer at the funerals of his unbelieving countrymen.

How did Caleb cope with the pressures of the wilderness? He learned contentment. At the age of seventy-nine he went into battle with Joshua and the conquering Israelites, fought in the war for six years, and at eighty-five claimed the high country Moses had promised him forty-six years before. After driving out the giants who lived there, Caleb turned the territory into his family homestead. That's a positive mental attitude nurtured by the lesson of contentment. With great fortitude and self-discipline Caleb waited for God to lead him into the Promised Land, regardless of the discomfort that preceded success.

Most people ruin today either by looking nostalgically back on the past or by peering so far into the future that they cannot enjoy the present.

Learn to relish today. The psalmist exclaimed, "This is the day which the LORD has made; let us rejoice and be glad in it" (Ps. 118:24, NASB). You may protest, "But I'm pregnant!" Enjoy your pregnancy and learn to be content, or some day you may lament, "But I have a baby [or two or four babies] on my hands." Learn to be content so you can take great delight in them, for the day may come when you will cry, "We now have three teenagers." Learn to enjoy them through thanksgiving, praise, and contentment, or some day you will fret, "My children have all gone, and I am bored; I wish I had them back."

Whether in the home or in business, many people have never learned contentment in the matters of time, talent, position, or money. They firmly believe that a change in circumstances will improve their lot, so they rush out and put themselves under financial bondage for a new home or a new car—only to find that it does not satisfy.

Since contentment is learned, why not learn it where you are? How? By thanking God for who He is and what He is doing in your life, then trusting Him for the future. You need goals—a subject for the next chapter—but don't forget to live today.

My godly grandmother used to say, "You can never give God tomorrow; you can only give Him today, because when tomorrow comes, it is suddenly today." Learn contentment in the present and "tomorrow" will seem much more friendly when it becomes "today."

SUMMARY

Let's summarize the four steps toward maintaining a good mental attitude. Rate yourself 0–25 (with 25 the highest) on each and see how close to 100 you score. Then work on the areas of your primary need.

1. Do you know who you are? _____
2. Do you accept yourself as God made you? _____
3. Have you developed a thanksgiving attitude? _____
4. Have you learned to be content where you are? _____

Total _____

If you do not score above 90, you really need to work consciously on your mental attitude. Read this chapter again and seek to practice its principles.

CHAPTER 10

How to Cope With Pressure

In 1923 a very important meeting was held in Chicago for nine of the world's most successful financiers. As presidents of major business enterprises, all the men had found the secret of "making big money." Twenty-five years later, media research on the nine men disclosed the following:

- The president of the largest independent steel company died in bankruptcy and lived on borrowed money for five years before his death;
- The president of the greatest utility company died a fugitive from justice and penniless in a foreign land;
- The president of the largest gas company went insane;
- The greatest wheat speculator died abroad insolvent;
- The president of the New York Stock Exchange had only recently been released from Sing Sing Prison;
- The former member of the President's cabinet was pardoned so he could die at home;
- The great "bear" on Wall Street died a suicide;
- The head of the greatest monopoly committed suicide;
- The president of the Bank of International Settlements was a suicide also.

All these men had learned the art of making a living, but apparently none of them had learned *how to live*.

These nine men clearly did not know how to handle pressure, but they are not alone. Millions like them have sought suicide as relief from pressure, and many more millions have been made ill by stress. Only God knows how many victims of ulcers, heart attacks, arthritis, and other diseases have suffered these physical problems because of pressure. Doctors have yet to invent an instrument that calibrates the amount of pressure a person is experiencing at a given time; they can measure only the effects of pressure. By the time a victim reaches the doctor's office, the effects invariably measure as negative.

We have already seen that pressure is unavoidable and evading it can be undesirable. In most instances pressure motivates strongly when properly controlled. If it doesn't, it becomes a negative force. But you never really want a pressure-free life, which would resemble living in a giant vacuum. Vacations are nice, but who wants to live on vacation fifty-two weeks a year? (Admittedly, this sounds appealing when pressure overwhelms us, but the people who live that way are not happy until they find something meaningful in which to invest their time.) You no doubt know of a businessman who worked toward retirement at age sixty-five, settled into his rocking chair, and either took his own life eighteen months later or died prematurely of natural causes.

Even unexpected pressure can be beneficial if we don't let it get out of control. An unplanned life is usually a very pressurized existence, just as an overplanned life intensifies pressure. The Bible teaches, "Let your moderation be known unto all men. The Lord is at hand" (Phil. 4:5, KJV).

The following guidelines or rules for handling pressure have helped me to cope with mine. I am confident they will serve you well.

ELEVEN STEPS TO CONTROLLING PRESSURE

1. DEVELOP A POSITIVE MENTAL ATTITUDE

The first step for controlling pressure is improving your mental attitude, as described in the preceding chapter. If you fail this test, all your pressures will be magnified. This doesn't mean you can't live with them, but they will certainly be more formidable than if you face them properly. It is impossible to exaggerate this point.

2. FIND THE WILL OF GOD FOR YOUR LIFE AND DO IT

If you don't discover something you consider meaningful to do with your life, meaningless activity will find you. Some women get "hooked on soaps," spending their prime time in a TV fantasy land of soap operas. Some men get "hooked on sports" (anything from golf, fishing, and spectator sports to poker).

God has designed this living machine we call one's total self (mind, soul, heart, and body) to work, serve, and be active. Those who selfishly protect themselves from this necessary activity suffer the pressure of self-rejection, purposeless living, and lack of accomplishment. You need to get involved with life and humanity, contributing to mankind during your time on earth. This truth may be why I have noticed a greater degree of peace within those who are in the people-helping business than in those who are not. Even non-Christians with the right mental attitude who are involved in serving others show fewer signs of pressure than Christians who live unto themselves.

Christians have a great advantage in this aspect of life, because they are challenged "to offer your bodies as living sacrifices, holy and pleasing to God—which is your spiritual worship" (Rom. 12:1, NIV). As they do so, they join that dedicated army of soldiers whose greatest joy comes from serving Jesus Christ. But the result of that life investment is enhanced, because it has an impact both in this life and the eternity to come.

As pastor I have found no greater cause with which to challenge young people than serving Christ. I have observed that many thousands who volunteer to serve Him do so for fifty and sometimes sixty years. As for work: Their cause is a lifetime challenge that motivates them long after others retire and after their bodies begin to wear out. Money, prestige, and fame do not motivate these people; they have given themselves to a cause that is greater than they are.

Early in my ministry I was impressed with the story of a veteran missionary to China in the early 1930s who was approached by a major oil company to represent it in an expansion plan. He knew the language of the people, was acculturized, and obviously had excellent rapport with the nationals. Four times they approached him, each time increasing the salary and benefit proposals. Finally, when they were offering him four times his missionary salary plus a strong retirement program, they asked, "What's wrong—is the salary too small?" He replied, "No, the job is too small!"

I take great satisfaction in knowing that I never have to fear coming to the end of life and finding that I have spent my days in secondary pursuits. I desire that for your life too. You may respond, "But I am not called to be a minister." That is not my point. You are called to "do the will of God." To some this may be a school board position, a state legislative post, or another public office. Is that serving Jesus Christ? Such individuals are called "ministers of God" three times in Romans 13. If you are a shoe salesman, homemaker, secretary, or laborer, ask not, "Is this a good profession for me?" but "Is this the will of God for me?"

If you are a Christian, finding the will of God for your life involves four factors: (1) The Word of God; (2) absolute obedience to it; (3) time; and (4) the Holy Spirit's guidance. Let's consider them briefly.

The Word of God. It is "a lamp to my feet and a light for my path" (Ps. 119:105, NIV). It will serve as an infallible guide. Examine these verses related to finding God's will.

> I will instruct you and teach you in the way you should go; I will counsel you and watch over you (Ps. 32:8, NIV).

> The LORD will guide you always; he will satisfy your needs in a sun-scorched land and will strengthen your frame. You will be like a well-watered garden, like a spring whose waters never fail (Isa. 58:11, NIV).

> Do not conform any longer to the pattern of this world, but be transformed by the renewing of your mind. Then you will be able to test and approve what God's will is—his good, pleasing and perfect will (Rom. 12:2, NIV).

Absolute obedience to the Word. God will not reveal more truth until we assimilate and implement His initial directions. John 14:21 says, "Whoever has my commands and obeys them, he is the one who loves me. He who loves me will be loved by my Father, and I too will love him and show myself to him"

(NIV). If you want God to manifest more truth to you in the future, then do what He has already told you in His Word.

Time. God is never in a hurry. He is eternal. Unfortunately we are impatient and excitable. In your eagerness to move ahead, always obey the instructions He has given today. Then wait on the Lord, be of good courage, and He will strengthen you for the task that lies ahead. But whenever you are asked to wait, serve Him where you are.

The most practical advice I ever received on this subject came from Dr. Bob Jones, Sr. He taught that life is like a series of rooms that need cleaning. Our job is to clean up the room we are in, after which God will open the door to another room that needs cleaning. Instead of worrying about our role next year or next month, we should occupy ourselves with cleaning today's room. God will provide the right place to serve Him in His good time. Later, after cleaning up a series of such rooms, we can look back and recognize how God has led us step by step. This finds accord with our Lord's promise that He is the God who opens: "What He opens, no one can shut; and what He shuts, no one can open" (Rev. 3:7, NIV).

The leading of the Holy Spirit. Some people claim that God speaks to them audibly or in visions. But He directs my life by "the still small voice" within me, the burden of my heart tested over a period of time. Here is one of my favorite verses regarding His leading:

> Let the peace of Christ rule in your hearts, since as members of one body you were called to peace. And be thankful. Let the Word of Christ dwell in you richly as you teach and admonish one another with all wisdom, and as you sing psalms, hymns and spiritual songs with gratitude in your hearts to God. And whatever you do, whether in word or deed, do it all in the name of the Lord Jesus, giving thanks to God the Father through Him (Col. 3:15–17, NIV).

Not all circumstances or opportunities in life are of God. Those that violate the Scriptures or do not glorify Jesus Christ are not even worth evaluating. God never leads us to violate His Word, and this is a principle that cannot be overemphasized. God is eternal, unchanging, and righteous; He is never the author of confusion. Any time a "spirit" suggests that you do anything that contradicts a biblical principle, it is not the Holy Spirit. According to the psalmist, "thou hast magnified thy word above all thy name" (Ps. 138:2, KJV). "Name" in reference to God means "nature," indicating that God regards His word above His very nature. Therefore you will never find God leading you contrary to the Bible.

D. L. Moody, the great evangelist of a past generation, used to say, "When I feel the urge to do something that does not violate biblical teachings, I accept it as the leading of God and do it with confidence." This is how "the peace of God" (Col. 3:15) can be the deciding factor. When the circumstances of life correspond with the Word of God and you have "peace" in your heart after praying about a matter, do it with "confidence" that it *is* His will.

We read in 1 John 5:14–15, "This is the assurance [confidence] we have in approaching God: that if we ask anything according to his will, he hears us. And if we know that he hears us—whatever we ask—we know that we have what we asked of him" (NIV). That confidence in heart is the greatest release for pressure in the world. Whenever you find yourself under pressure, yet able to take stock of events that placed you there and to honestly say, "I know God has led me," it is a tremendous relief from the distress caused by pressure. And it can be an exhilarating source of positive motivation.

Most pastors "honeymoon" at a new church for from six months to two years. During that time the congregation knows he can "do no wrong." This was not my experience, however. Beverly and I came to Scott Memorial Church in San Diego when I was thirty years old and still very inexperienced. The church was forty-four years old and "very set in its ways." My honeymoon lasted six weeks! I will never forget waking up to the fact that this lovely congregation had deep-seated denominational and philosophical divisions. For more than five years we experienced conflict between the liberal element devoted to denominational loyalty and the conservatives committed to doctrinal purity. I was caught in the middle: Committed to doctrinal purity on the one hand, and the preservation of the love, unity, and harmony of the local church on the other. During those years transient families—many of them fulfilling two-year tours of duty for the navy—came to church every Sunday and never realized that this turmoil was boiling. But I knew it! There was real pressure! Yet many times I recalled the specific leading of God that had originally produced an affirmative vote of 97 percent of the congregation to our call. (Bev and I had asked for at least 95 percent.)

Looking back after twenty-five years, I could firmly say that God led us to that ministry. But we were sure of that even amid the pressurized years, and this knowledge eased the pressure. Anytime you leave the will of God, you can expect even ordinary pressure to be multiplied, and you will not experience "peace with God." Don't settle for less than the perfect will of God for your life.

3. COMMIT YOURSELF TO BASIC VALUES AND STICK YOURSELF TO THEM

"Situation ethics," the philosophy of morality advocated by the secular, elite educators for forty years, leads to both an unbiblical and an unhappy lifestyle. This high-sounding approach of waiting until you get into a situation to decide whether a policy can be deemed right or wrong is so psychologically unsound that it accentuates pressure instead of easing it. I am convinced that many of our depression-caused suicides are victims of such a lifestyle.

Throughout life you will be pressured by people or circumstances to adapt your values or principles to "current trends" or modern ideas. Such tampering with the social and moral absolutes of God intensifies life's pressures. Consider one young couple who came for counseling. Their marriage relationship was admittedly weak, and this produced considerable pressure. To this was added the husband's adultery. Through the clenched teeth of anger the wife began, "He gave me Herpes ." That is pressure compounded by the wages of sin.

If ever there was an age when commitment to basic moral values is needed, it is ours. The pressures on young and old alike are greater than they have ever been. You cannot decide for the entire culture in which you live, but you can decide for yourself, for the kind of people with whom you associate, and for those whom you vote into public office. The movement toward liberal lifestyles and self-indulgent sinful practices is beginning to wane. An article in *U.S. News and World Report* (July 1982) indicated that the permissiveness of the last four decades is giving way to a fixed standard of morality in opposition to drugs, crime, abortion, and even the expulsion of God and prayer from our public schools.

Daniel the prophet has been the exemplary figure of all time in regard to public morality. He totally refused to compromise his basic values. At age seventeen it was said of him, "Daniel purposed in his heart that he would not defile himself" with the king's food or drink (Dan. 1:8). He endured intense pressure to compromise, but he refused to succumb. It is not surprising that seventy years later under different circumstances he again refused to compromise, even though that meant being thrown into the lion's den.

We admire Daniel's courage and strength of character, but that doesn't tell the whole story. Men and women of great courage have sometimes given way when confronted with pressure. The difference with Daniel, besides his spiritual strength, was his commitment to moral values. This adherence to personal and public values should be an integral part of all teaching in home and church. Parents who do not share God's basic values with their children are not preparing them adequately for life. What *are* these basic values? Consider the commandments that God gave to Israel, all reiterated in the New Testament.

- Love God with all your heart, mind and soul.
- Do not bow down to images.
- Do not take God's name in vain.
- Love your neighbor as yourself.
- Honor your parents.
- Do not kill.
- Do not commit adultery.
- Do not steal.
- Do not lie.
- Do not covet.

People who adopt this basic standard for living and refuse to deviate from it are happier, more successful, and much less pressured in life than those who pursue a relativistic course.

Ed Heacock was a builder of beautiful custom homes in our

city. Several years before he died of cancer, he accepted Jesus Christ as his Lord and Savior, and the experience revolutionized his life. One day I asked him, "Ed, what changes have you noticed in your life since you became a Christian?" He replied, "The way I go to the telephone. In fact, I was thinking of it last night as my son called me to the phone to talk to a woman for whom I am building a house. Previously I would be racking my brain, trying to recall what I had said in our last conversation. Instead, I walked calmly to the phone, knowing that whatever she asked, I would give the same answer I did last time—*the truth.*"

Sometimes "the truth hurts," but in the long run it eases the pressure of difficult decisions. I have found that a commitment to truth simplifies most of life's decisions. In the organizations I have headed, I solved difficult problems many times by simply asking, "What is right?" When it involves the basic moral values to which we have committed ourselves, the answer is usually quite simple.

During your lifetime you will be tempted to do wrong. Some temptations look very appealing—but they are still wrong. Evaluating them in the light of your commitment to do right, regardless of extenuating circumstances, will both simplify your life and reduce your pressures. At other times doing right will intensify external pressures exerted by those who seek to make you compromise. The confidence that you are doing right will so ease your inner pressures that you will be able to cope with those outside. And when you look at your reflection in the mirror, you won't have to hang your head.

Before you read further, make a list of the basic values, people, and causes to which you have committed yourself. Much of your self-respect in life will be fulfilled by keeping that commitment.

More than thirty years ago I made a personal, moral, financial, and spiritual commitment to an eighteen-year-old woman who became my wife. As we celebrate our anniversary each year, I recall that commitment. Through the years there have been a few minor temptations—minor since they were never given serious consideration, because they violated my basic commitments. Consequently we have been spared the grief, guilt, remorse, and unhappiness that is so common with many our age.

4. SET HIGH, CLEARLY DEFINED, AND REASONABLE GOALS AND COMMIT YOURSELF TO THEM

"He who aims at nothing will be sure to hit it," Henrietta O. Mears once wrote. In my opinion, there is no pressure comparable to personal failure in life. The most miserable people I know are those who fail in their own eyes. This failure is like a quagmire that engulfs them. By contrast, I have noticed that personal satisfaction with living is usually the salient feature of longevity.

Hans Selye emphasizes, "Whatever goals we strive for, the relationship between stress and the attainment of our aims is so evident that it hardly justifies lengthy discussions. *Mental tensions, frustrations, insecurity,* and *aimlessness* are among the most damaging stressors, and psychosomatic studies have shown how often they cause *migraine headaches, peptic ulcers, heart attacks, hypertension, mental disease, suicide,* or just hopeless unhappiness" (emphasis added).[1] He further states, "To remain healthy, man must have some goal, some purpose in life that he can respect and be proud to work for. Each person must work out a way to relieve his pent-up energy without creating conflicts with his fellow men and, if possible, to earn their goodwill and respect."[2]

Unmotivated people are goal-less people. We have already observed that the apostle Paul was a highly motivated person. Scripture shows that he was also a very goal-oriented man. So is everyone else who accomplishes anything in life, from social work to engineering to professional sports.

Life goals are usually based on one's philosophy of life. Secular humanists with their atheistic philosophy do not believe in life after death; consequently their life goals are confined to this earth and their lifetime. To a Christian the ultimate goal is eternal, and his commitment to that view will

---

[1] Selye, *Stress Without Distress*, 111.
[2] Ibid., 103.

motivate him for more than a lifetime. Perhaps this is why so many Christians are disinterested in retirement.

Even Christians, however, can have unmotivated lives due to inadequate or harmful goals. Ironically the absence of goals does not reduce your pressure, but increases it, for you find yourself pressured into conforming to other people's goals. That will be valuable only if their goals pqrallel yours.

THREE KINDS OF GOALS

We can identify three basic kinds of goals, each related to distance or time. You will experience these time zones in life, so it is good to lay clearly defined plans for them as a means of reducing the normal pressures of living.

Short-Term Goals

Short-term goals usually provide immediate gratification: Food, shelter, exercise, pleasure, or the culmination of long-range goals now being realized. All these create their own kinds of pressure. Many people get so involved in the pressures generated by these necessary goals that they seldom, if ever, look beyond them. Most of them are pressed upon us through everyday living, but if this is all life affords, it can become quite boring. Usually little training is required to realize these short-term goals, but they are necessary to all living. They become dangerous only if we should concentrate on them so exclusively that they become our only goals.

Since short-term goals provide instant gratification, many unwise people are consumed by them. Many never complete their education or make the long-range plans or sacrifices necessary to improve their lot in life. Such people rarely read a book like this one. They create much unnecessary pressure for themselves by their inattention to more pertinent goals.

A young sports car enthusiast endured a job he despised so he could spend his evenings working on sport and racing cars in his garage. It eventually cost him his wife and eighteen-month-old son, whom he ignored to indulge in his hobby. Others have done the same with athletics, entertainment, and gambling. Short-term goals are necessary, but they do not encompass all of life.

Long-Term Goals

What do you plan to do next year? Five years from now? In a decade? Don't just say, "The Lord's will" or "Whatever God leads me to do." These answers may be correct, but they can best be realized as you make plans to move in that direction now. A housewife needs a husband, children, and home. To achieve those goals, think positively about them and begin prayerfully to make plans for their realization now. I have found that God can steer a moving automobile more easily than one that is parked.

"Waiting on God," a biblical truism heard many times, does not mean sitting back and waiting for God to do everything for you. Joshua and the children of Israel had to march around the city of Jericho seven times while "waiting on God" to give them the victory. The Israelites under Joshua had to fight six years of war while "waiting on God" to give them the Promised Land. David had to flee for his life from Saul and live in caves while "waiting on God" to gain the kingdom. I have had to hold more than two hundred fund-raising banquets or seminars while "waiting on the Lord" to provide the financial base needed to launch a national television ministry. "Waiting on God" usually involves hard work.

Nehemiah discovered this truth. God did not give the children of Israel clear title to the land with a newly walled city after they returned from their Babylonian captivity. They had to build the wall block by block with a spear in one hand—ready to fight their Canaanite enemies—and a trowel in the other. When it was completed, Nehemiah said, "So we built a wall, and the entire wall was joined together up to half its height, for the people had a mind to work" (Neh. 4:6, NKJ). One day back in Babylon that wall was merely a vision or goal in the mind of Nehemiah, but he kept his mind on it in prayer. After requesting permission of the king to leave Babylon, he laid his plans, gathered the people and supplies, traveled, worked, and sacrificed—and then gave God the glory.

I too have found that "waiting on the Lord" requires a lot of work. My wife has suggested, "Perhaps work is God's method of pruning us to see how sincere we really are." Nothing comes without hard work—nothing worthwhile, that is. Whenever I see someone playing the piano, I say wistfully, "I wish I could learn to play the piano." But that is not really ture. Actually I am wishing that God would zap me with a miracle so that suddenly, without effort, I am transformed into an accomplished pianist.

"Resting in the Lord" does not mean physical rest; you should expect it to be strenuous work. It is important to realize this at the beginning of any project. When you drive past a beautiful church building and remark, "The Lord has given this congregation a marvelous facility to worship in," you are only partially right. "Every good and perfect gift comes from God," we are told in James 1:17; but God did not do for those people what He expected them to do for themselves. After their pastor received the vision, they elected the committees, confronted the city planners, and overcame anti-church neighbors who oppose all church expansion. Then they planned the financial campaign, received the pledges, and sacrificially "gave unto the Lord." Finally, after two to six years of planning and hard work while "resting in the Lord," the congregation finished its new building—so they could continue their service, grow, and eventually have the privilege of repeating the entire process again in ten years. That's "resting in God."

We all enjoy the finished product, but we must always remember that someone developed the initial program, turned it into a goal through planning, and then started to work toward it.

YOUTHFUL FLOYD AT AGE 74

Beverly and I recently spent a night with her eighty-four-year-old mother and her new husband of six months in their retirement village in Sebring, Florida. When I was introduced to speak at the midweek prayer service, more than five hundred people filled a beautiful new church building. I had jogged my way through their park that afternoon and had marveled at the two lakes, boats, tour bus, fire engine and station house, and other incredibly convenient features. I remarked, "Nothing so good just happens; this place must be the fulfilled dream of some person." The audience spontaneously applauded and then pointed to the young-looking man managing the sound control board.

As we went out for coffee later, I found Floyd to be an exciting seventy-four-year-old visionary. It took only a few questions to discover that he had been a building contractor in Michigan who dreamed of constructing a retirement community for Christians to enjoy during the twilight years of life. As he thought and prayed, his vision began to take on the dimension of a goal through planning. Finally he found a 225-acre-site, formulated architectural plans, spent two years dealing with local, county, and state agencies, and worked for two more years in building the village. I was looking into the face of a healthy, fulfilled, and involved "retired" contractor. I came away from there saying to Bev, "When I'm seventy-four, I'd like to be just like Floyd."

Goals and plans always create pressure, but they fashion the positive pressure that motivates us to accomplishment.

What goals do you have? After making a list, write each goal on a sheet of paper and enumerate all the steps you can think of that are necessary to fulfill that goal. Then start prioritizing these items.

THE SECRET OF GOAL MOTIVATION

As we saw in the chapter on temperaments, some people are more analytical than others. Because melancholies are extremely analytical, they can readily lay out long lists of steps necessary to accomplish their goals. They tend to incorporate so much detail, however, that they discourage themselves and often abandon projects. Being a choleric/sanguine by nature, I am goal-oriented, but not very analytical. So I have developed a special secret for helping me analyze in advance the steps necessary to fulfillment of those goals: Concentration on the goals, and extensive discussion of them with my friends.

Concentrate on Your Goals

Just as you adjust the knobs on the TV set, you need to focus in on your goals with your God-given imagination. At the beginning they will seem so distant that you will barely see them. But keep looking. The more you concentrate on them, the better they will focus, and gradually your subconscious mind will surface thoughts that will enable you to achieve your goals. It is important to write down the goals; later you can sort through them. Even when it would seem that all is lost, don't fail to scrutinize your visions until they turn into goals. I have found jogging to be a great occasion to meditate with God and massage my goals. My wife can testify that after returning from jogging, I often reach for my pen to write down some thought before it steals away.

Talk Your Vision Out Till It Turns Into a Goal

By sharing visions and goals with your friends, you will benefit from their thinking. Many of my best goals have been sharpened by the comments of associates. Beware, however, the professional negativist and the perennial critic; the former will always register a million reasons why your plan will fail, because his regularly fall flat. Just remember, there are two kinds of people: Those who think they can, and those who think they can't. They are both right. Don't waste your time introducing your visions to negative friends, for they rarely contribute anything positive. To them, goals are enemy missiles to be shot out of the sky.

Beware also the perennial critic. His egomania compels him to discourage and find fault with everything positive. Your success becomes a burden to his repeated failure. You will soon learn who can be trusted to fairly appraise, solidify, and augment your goals.

Except for the two types of people "whose speech betrays them" because it is so critical or negative, share your ideas freely. Some of your friends will inevitably contribute positive suggestions, and their input can propel you toward realizing your goals.

There is one other practice I find helpful. I like to drift off to sleep talking to God. That isn't my devotional life; I just like to converse with my heavenly Father as the day comes to a close. Rarely do I discuss with Him the activities of tomorrow (unless I am to preach a new sermon or have a special interview). Putting tomorrow out of my mind, I usually drift off to sleep focusing upon and talking to God about my long-range goals and visions. Goals are usually one month to five years away, visions from five to ten years. Actually, I have devised so many visions and goals that I have only to rehearse a handful of them before dropping off to sleep. When my head is filled with future aspirations, who needs to count sheep? With great satisfaction I find that some of my visions and goals of fifteen years ago are now on-going agencies, organizations, programs, or buildings.

I discovered a secret long ago. We ordinary people need all the help we can get and more. Visualizing goals will produce those miraculous results we all want to see accomplished.

What about eternal goals?

Identify Your Ultimate Goals

Your basic philosophy of life will often determine your ultimate, or eternal, goals. If you ask a typical Christian about his ultimate goals, you will receive a series of heartwarming responses. Consider some I have received:

- "To go to heaven when I die"
- "To enjoy my Lord forever"
- "To sing God's praises forever"
- "To cast my crowns at Jesus' feet"
- "To walk the streets of gold"
- "To live in the heavenly city"
- "To continue serving Him in the Millennium and throughout eternity"
- "To see my entire family in heaven"
- "To hear my Lord say, 'Well done, thou good and faithful servant, enter into the joy of the Lord' "
- "Just to see the Lord and my loved ones again"

No person can establish ultimate goals unless he has a deep conviction concerning life after death. Written on the table of every man's heart is the conviction that life is eternal. Both the Old and New Testaments affirm this truth. The further a person strays from the Word of God, the less his life will be motivated by eternal values. The closer he remains to the Word, the more real will be his belief in eternity; ultimate goals will naturally follow.

For example, on the day that I was writing this section, my

devotions included Psalm 136, where twenty-six times it is written, "His mercy endureth *forever*." With this kind of reaffirmation, it is not difficult to think long-range, no matter what your vocation. Two men discussed their future plans with me on the same day; both were Christians preparing to retire from business. The first talked about vacations, fishing, travel, and leisure—nothing eternal. The second man couldn't wait to have more free time to serve the Lord. He wanted to know if I could teach him some counseling techniques so he could serve as a telephone counselor for our television program.

The most fulfilled people are those who have such an abiding confidence in ultimate life after death and our eventual meeting with God that they live their whole lives with this in view. They can say with Paul, "I have fought the good fight, I have finished the race, I have kept the faith. Now there is in store for me the crown of righteousness, which the Lord, the righteous Judge, will award to me on that day—and not only to me, but also to all who have longed for his appearing" (2 Tim. 4:7–8, NIV). Daniel Webster, the great American statesman, was asked, "Mr. Webster, what is the greatest thought that ever went through your mind?" He replied, "My accountability to God."

Always keep in mind that ultimate or eternal goals are not just for the gifted, creative, or "full-time Christian worker." They are for everyone, for God is so just that He will mete out eternal rewards in direct proportion to our time, talents, and opportunities. Keep your eye on the eternal goal and let God apply the positive pressure that motivates you to serve Him. As you look to the eternal, His Spirit will supply more than enough ultimate goals to serve as lifetime targets.

Make Your Goals Reasonable

The human mind, like a computer, rejects the impossible. If you set unreasonable goals, you will only frustrate yourself. Be practical. Allow for the dimension of God's power, but don't waste time on foolish or fruitless goals. For instance, it would be folly for me to envision myself a professional basektball player or a portrait artist (I couldn't even paint a house), but a writer—that's different. I enjoyed writing letters long before I tried to formulate a book. Many of my friends claimed that they enjoyed receiving my letters, so writing books became a reasonable goal. Designing a house? Never! In fact, all of us would find many goals unreasonable.

Avoid the crushing disappointment of shattered dreams by letting the Lord help you to establish your goals. Psalm 37:4 admonishes, "Delight yourself in the LORD and he will give you the desires of your heart" (NIV). I have found that whenever a dream or vision begins to materialize, I pray earnestly about it. First, I yield it to Him; life is too short to spend time chasing rainbows. If the vision or burden or desire persists, God usually brings people, events, and His Word into focus to confirm the vision. Before long, the vision becomes a distinct goal.

Keep watching, praying, planning, and talking about it. Gradually the goal takes on material substance, and the moment comes when, like Peter, you are compelled to take that big step out of the boat and onto the water. Don't look down at the problems, which only increase the pressure that all new projects generate. You will sink under the waves, engulfed by perplexities and uncertainties. By "looking unto Jesus the author and finisher of our faith" (Heb. 12:2, KJV). He knows the end from the beginning. Like Peter, when you feel the water around your knees, cry, "Lord! save me!" He will!

Dawson Trotman, the founder of Navigators and a man who had trusted God for the fulfillment of his visionary goals, once said, "Attempt such things for God that if He fails you, you're sunk." I know that feeling. It's truly exciting to know that if God took His hand away for one second, you would sink out of sight. It's not really difficult to be spiritual at such times. You resort continually to the Word and of necessity pray without ceasing. That represents a profitable use of pressure. But whatever the test of faith, who wants to ride in a boat when God invites us to walk on water?

5. SEEK THE ADVICE OF COMPETENT PEOPLE

No one is clever enough to fulfill a major role in life all by himself. I find that humble people are not reluctant to ask for help. They realize that life is so complex today that they must ask the counsel of experts in fields outside their own. In his inimitable way, Dr. Bob Jones used to urge, "If you don't have brains, borrow them from those who do."

The Bible says, "For the lack of guidance a nation falls, but many advisers make victory sure" (Prov. 11:14, NIV). King Rehoboam, however, found that just seeking the aid of counselors was not enough. To his detriment, he selected only those who would give him the advice he wanted, and ultimately this approach cost him the kingdom (see 1 Kings 12). It is better to seek and require three qualities from your counselors.

Seek the aid of spiritual counselors. The psalmist said, "Blessed is the man that walketh *not* in the counsel *of the ungodly*" (Ps. 1:1, KJV). I have been appalled to discover that many Christian parents will naively heed the counsel of educators (the typical Ph.D. "professionally trained guidance counselor") for the future education or vocation of their children. Such people need to understand that "man's ways are not my ways, saith the Lord" (See Isa. 55:8–9).

> For who among men knows the thoughts of a man except the man's spirit within him? In the same way no one knows the thoughts of God except the Spirit of God. We have not received the spirit of the world but the Spirit who is from God, that we may understand what God has freely given us. This is what we speak, not in words taught us by human wisdom but in words taught by the Spirit, expressing spiritual truths in spiritual words. The man without the Spirit does not accept the things that come from the Spirit of God, for they are foolishness to him, and he cannot understand them, because they are spiritually discerned. The spiritual man makes judgments about all things, but he himself is not subject to any man's judgment: "For who has known the mind of the Lord that he may instruct him?" But we have the mind of Christ (1 Cor. 2:11–16, NIV).

The first criterion in seeking counsel, then, is a person's spiritual qualifications.

Seek the advice of capable, experienced professionals. Some needed advice will be so technical that it will require a very well-trained person to provide counsel. This is certainly true of the medical profession. I would not ask a carpenter or computer expert to advise me concerning the physical maladies of my family. Savor the advice of a counselor in the light of his competence. Sometimes you may need the guidance of a lawyer or architect who is not a Christian. Just be certain to evaluate his views with that in mind.

Seek a counselor who is objective. Objectivity in a counselor is simply the ability to be impersonal. It may be difficult for a salesman to be objective about your purchase of his product, or a neighbor to be objective about what you should do with your barking dog. You need a counselor who is free to give you the best advice possible without being personally involved.

It is very difficult to know how objective another person really is. For this reason, seek advice from spiritually minded people who submit themselves to the Word of God, competent to give that counsel and with as objective a viewpoint as possible. But when all is said and done, *you* will have to make the final decision. Gather the evidence, carefully consider all the ramifications, seek the leading of God, commit yourself to Him, and then follow your inner urgings.

6. WORK OUT A CLEARLY DEFINED PLAN FOR ACHIEVING YOUR GOALS

Much of the excessive pressure people experience stems from poor planning. Some of it ensues from the absence of planning. Here is a practical rule: The better the plan, the less the pressure. Yes, there will be surprises, no matter how sound your plan; but a thoroughly developed blueprint will protect you from most surprises and allow you to absorb the pressures caused by the unexpected.

Observing an architect can be instructive. Most of his training he's in the discipline of planning. Our church architect made several sketches, renderings, and designs before he ever started his detailed drawings. A large project will generate a flood of paper on the floor of your architect's office. But that kind of planning saves money, time, delays, and pressure-induced headaches.

Whenever you must transform a goal into a plan, write down your thoughts on paper. Keep a note pad by your bed, on your desk, and even in the car. I am an inveterate 3x5 card carrier. Such a device greatly assists the planning process.

7. CAREFULLY COUNT THE COST AND DETERMINE A REASONABLE PLAN FOR MEETING IT

The Bible challenges us to live by faith. I have launched many projects by faith, but faith is no excuse for foolishness. We have all heard "the Lord's will" get the blame for someone's inept planning. That only brings reproach to the cause of Christ. If God leads you to launch out by faith, He will also provide a plan for paying the bills.

I know of a church that enjoys a beautiful facility with a half-filled auditorium each Sunday. The congregation is $4 million in debt and was forced to borrow money this year to pay the interest on the bonds in order to avoid receivership. Contrast this with a Christian college worth millions operating at capacity enrollment. It refuses to start any project until God provides money in advance. Its administrators feel that it takes more faith to trust God for the money in advance than to build on credit and then "cry wolf" afterward.

I like the college plan for two reasons: (1) It is a noteworthy testimony to God's provision, and (2) it doesn't waste God's money on high interest payments. At least half their present buildings were constructed on the interest savings that otherwise would have gone to the bankers.

Financial planning helps to offset undue pressure. The Bible teaches that a wise man counts the cost before building (e.g., Luke 14:28–30). Many of the families I counsel are assailed by exorbitant house payments, car payments, and other high-interest credit purchases. It is better to live in humble circumstances without pressure than in a lovely home whose payments create a monthly pressure on the family budget.

Every family should have a budget. But I find that many Christians have never taken the time to prepare one. You will be amazed at the amount of pressure and tension you can ease by proper budgeting. It may seem like a "bother" at the time, but it will help you sleep better. Nevertheless, don't prepare a budget unless you intend to follow it. Avoid purchases that cause you to nullify your carefully devised control system.

8. LEARN TO BE A NOTE TAKER

Unless you have a photographic memory, you will seriously hinder your potential and unnecessarily increase life's usual pressures if you are not a note taker. I have facetiously told my friends that I have a photographic memory; I seldom admit that I can never remember where I put the film. Thus I continue to carry 3x5 cards wherever I go.

Life's details have increased at a dizzying pace during the past decade, accelerating the demands placed on us. I have watched many capable people seriously limit themselves because they refuse to jot down ideas, responsibilities, and future plans. I find the simple act of writing things down a way of more deeply impressing a matter on my mind, making it less likely that I will forget it.

One technique I find helpful is to list unfinished tasks on a card, using the face side for my "A" section, meaning priorities today. The back of the card is reserved for "B" (tomorrow) and "C" (future) commitments. As I complete each project, I draw a line through it. Each night I prepare a new card, transferring the appropriate B or C activities to the A section. The entire process takes only a few minutes, but it is very relaxing, particularly as I prepare for bed, to know that all unfinished activity is mapped out properly. It relieves my mind from the pressure of unsettled responsibilities.

Bev has also become a list maker. As the responsibilities of Concerned Women for America have increased, her workload at the office has also grown. In addition, she is working on another book and has traveled with me all year as co-host of our TV program. We laugh at each other as we get ready for a trip. If we fail to write down all responsibilities before leaving town, we will leave a trail of unfinished work all over the country. Therefore, keeping a list helps us to avoid one of the worst pressures we face—remembering some important phone call or duty as our plane is taking off for a 3,000-mile trip across three time zones. My little cards and Bev's lists are great pressure relievers.

9. ESTABLISH PROPER PRIORITIES FOR DAILY LIVING

Everyone has the same amount of time—twenty-four hours a day. I am convinced that successful people don't work much harder than ordinary people or the unsuccessful; they simply spend their time more wisely. During the last few years Bev and I have placed a healthy emphasis on priorities. I have already indicated that the proper basic priorities according to the Bible are (1) God; (2) partner; (3) family; and (4) vocation. Daily priorities reflect these basics if you set them on your daily card or note pad.

Most people live their lives like Ping-Pong balls being batted back and forth by someone else's paddle. Because they are "busy," they mistakenly consider themselves productive. You will find that if you don't plan your own agenda, other people will plan it for you; then you will experience all kinds of pressure, because your own priorities or needs are not being fulfilled.

This is why keeping a calendar of future engagements and duties is absolutely necessary. Daily and weekly planning sessions allow you to enter your priorities on your schedule before someone else does. If you ask me to speak on July 5, for instance, I will rarely accept, for I have a lifetime priority date with my wife: It's our anniversary. When our children were home, I scheduled Thursday evenings and Saturdays as "family days." When people asked for engagements on those dates, I could honestly say, "I'm sorry, but I have an appointment." Otherwise I would have been pressured out of priority time with my children.

As a busy pastor I found it difficult to have sufficient time for writing. I solved this by remaining in my study from 8:00 to 11:30 each morning to study with "no interruptions." Few emergencies were so great that I could not handle them in the afternoon during my administrative time. Thursday was always writing day. I didn't answer the phone, open the front door, or accept appointments. Wednesday night I read myself full; all day Thursday I wrote myself empty.

Inevitably, I irritated some people who demanded to see me on *their* priority list "right now." But since I am not a doctor and my patients don't usually face life-threatening emergencies, I prefer to let them fit into *my* priority schedule. Today millions of copies of my books are in print, ministering to people all over the world in more than eighteen languages; that would never have happened had I not established the priority of writing on a given day. Other people would have planned my agenda, and I would have fit in with their plans instead of doing what for me became top priority.

Mothers often feel a loss as their children leave the home, because those youngsters have established the parental agenda for years. Now that the children are gone, mother has nothing to do. By properly planning your own daily agenda over the years, you will find that Johnny's "graduation day" is a graduation day for both mother and child.

The more active your life, the more important the daily priorities are. If you fail to set them, you will find yourself adjusting to other people's plans, working harder, and feeling more pressure because you are not getting your priority work finished. One reason businessmen bring their work home, is that, forfeiting their own priorities at the office, they were "pressured" into miscellaneous activities, creating work pressure at home at the expense of the family.

10. TAKE TIME TO LOVE OTHERS

You are not a machine. Your body may function like a well-oiled human machine, but you are more than a body. The total "you" includes mind, soul, *heart*, and body. You neglect your heart at your peril. Man is an emotional creature with the capacity to share his emotions with another. Everyone needs someone with whom he can share his life; God has planned that someone to be your mate. But because of death, divorce, sin, and a host of other problems, His plan may be short-circuited. Consequently you need a best friend, many close friends, and a larger sphere of other friends.

Our Lord loved all people, but enjoyed various levels of friendship. His closest intimates were Peter, James, and John. He spent more time with them and invested more of Himself and His love in them than in any of His other followers. So it will be with you. Those to whom you extend your love will

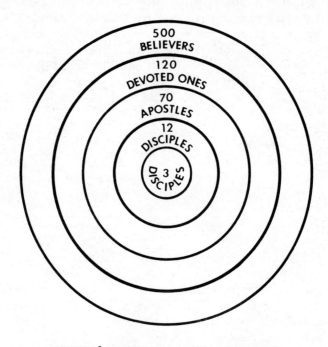

JESUS' SPHERE OF FRIENDS

usually return it. But love takes time, involvement, and sacrifice. It is a worthy investment of your life and deserves a lofty rating on your priority list. Some people may not return your love, but that is their loss. Your responsibility is to give love, not accrue it.

Give for the joy of giving. Take time to express love, friendliness and personal interest to those you love, those who can never return your love, and those who are just passing through your life once and may need someone's love. And be sure to bestow love upon those who hate or oppose you. I admire Francis A. Schaeffer for his infectious challenge of showing compassion to those who oppose and despise him. He hates humanism, for instance, but he loves the individual secular humanist. Love is truly the key to fulfillment in life.

11. KEEP THE LIGHT BURNING
AT THE END OF THE TUNNEL

We have already seen that pressure is intensified when hope is lacking. No one can live very long without hope. In fact, without hope there is no faith. The Bible says, "Faith is the substance of things hoped for" (Heb. 11:1). Our belief in Jesus' second coming is called "the Blessed Hope." That doesn't mean it is doubtful, as in "I hope He will come again." "Hope" in the Bible represents a confident expectation based on faith. The saddest position in the world is existence in a state of hopelessness.

When the light of hope flickers and is then extinguished, you will feel the greatest of all pressure. I have experienced this vicariously many times with people who have lost loved ones; were rejected by parents, spouse or friend; were devastated by a divorce; or in some cases were forsaken for another "lover." For these souls, the light at the end of their tunnel had been snuffed out temporarily. As a Christian counselor I always tried to help them rekindle that light.

One biblical principle is essential to maintaining mental health: "Where there is no vision the people perish" (Prov. 29:18, KJV). If the light at the end of your tunnel has gone out, I know that your pressures have become unbearable. But I have good news for you: Throughout the Bible God delivers messages of hope to His despairing children. This past year I have been dependent on that source more than at any time in my life, and I am happy to report that it is a "very present help in time of need." I devote the last chapter of this book to the subject of what to do when the light at the end of your tunnel goes out. But first we must examine some physical ways to relieve pressure. These are not so long lasting as the means of handling pressure discussed in chapter 12, but they are valuable and may save your life someday.

CHAPTER 11

Physical Relief From Pressure

Billy Graham unwittingly started me jogging back in 1966. In a *Reader's Digest* article published some three years after he inaugurated a jogging program, he explained how the activity had helped him physically. In his mid-forties Graham had developed a string of minor ailments, was vulnerable to colds and flu, and was constantly tired in the late afternoon. Soon after he began jogging, his physical maladies cleared up and he felt better than he had in years. He was so convincing in the article that I started jogging the next day and have continued to the present. I now jog three miles on five or more days each week when I am home and as often as possible when I am traveling.

Little did I realize when I started the program that it would prove to be an excellent means to relieve pressure. I am convinced that when I was going through my most severe pressures, jogging could have been a lifesaver. Each morning as I went to the track to push my body through its twenty-five-minute workout, I felt that I was carrying the weight of the world on my back. Before I finished, my spirits were lifted, a surge of optimism had swept over me, and I had enjoyed a long talk with my heavenly Father. Before I had finished those twelve laps, He had relit the light at the end of my tunnel.

Jogging isn't the only answer for relieving pressure, of course. My research has uncovered seven steps, all of them vital. Use them to greatly increase your ability to withstand pressure.

1. PRACTICE PROPER DAILY NUTRITION

What gasoline is to a car, food is to the human body. Buy cheap gas and your car's engine will ping, function sluggishly, and generally perform below its capabilities. Feed your body junk food and you will live to regret it, particularly when you discover what it will do to your emotions. Remember, what you are emotionally is what you are. And the food you eat affects your emotions.

A nationally famous medical doctor noted something fascinating in his best-selling book on saving one's life through diet. He considered it bizarre that in America we purchase our food from two kinds of stores, health stores and "unhealthy" stores. Most people have patronized the unhealthy stores because the prices were cheaper, but now the big chain supermarkets have responded to our national movement toward health food and are gradually adding products that are healthful to their customers. But even then one must be a discerning buyer lest he feed his family junk food.

As a pastor I have watched various fads sweep through a congregation, many of them having to do with food. Friends have given me books, pamphlets, and printed lectures in countless number, and I have read them carefully. I even subscribed to *Prevention* magazine for twenty years, until the editor died of a heart attack at age seventy-two. I know people who have lived long beyond that age who didn't take vitamins and broke many rules of healthful eating. Consequently I have made a few observations, programmed them into my "mental computer," and produced my own theory of health. I urge you to evaluate it at your risk, for I am not a medical doctor.

Here are some considerations to ponder regarding food:

• Processed foods such as anything with white flour and white sugar are unnatural. Tests show that cancer and other serious illnesses have increased in civilized societies since the advent of processed foods. Some backward countries that lack processed foods have not yet acquired some of the health hazards so prominent in the more developed countries.

• People who take vitamins claim to feel better and assert that vitamins have helped them overcome certain maladies.

• On the other hand, many sickly people take vitamins. I haven't noticed much difference in the spread of infectious diseases between nutrition-eaters and junk-food addicts. Healthfood people seem more anxious and obsessed with such subjects as pesticides, fertilizers, and nutrients. I would prefer that they be preoccupied with the ministry of the Holy Spirit and service to Jesus Christ. They would be far more relaxed and might even outlive some of their church friends who thrive on junk food.

• The life-expectancy rate has been rising and people are growing taller during the very years junk food has been prominent. I can't believe that our current wave of six-foot-ten basketball players has all been raised on goat's milk, peanuts, and lotus leaves.

• The medical profession is generaly hostile to taking vitamin supplements. The "experts" don't agree on the subject, and Ph.D and M.D. degrees can be cited on either side to make a case for taking no vitamins or taking megavitamins.

SIMPLE RULES FOR GOOD NUTRITION

Because scientific experts cannot agree, the Bible speaks to the subject only in a limited way, and we still must eat to live, we should set reasonable rules and trust God to take care of us and our families. Here are the rules I have followed for many years while enjoying extremely good health. (Except for Bev's arthritis, none of our family of six has ever suffered a serious ailment.)

• Eat plenty of fruits, vegetables, and other natural foods.

• Avoid white sugar and white flour whenever possible; abstain from foods high in carbohydrates and cholesterol.

• Eat plenty of whole-grain products.

• Limit your consumption of beef to once or twice a week, avoid ham entirely, and eat fish and fowl.

• Limit or exclude sweets from your diet.

• Take a multiple vitamin daily, and consume extra quantities of the B complex and C, particularly during times of pressure. I prefer natural vitamins time-released rather than synthetic supplements; the former tend to remain in the body longer. During my times of greatest pressure I am careful to take a special time-released combination of the B complex and C called "super-stress 600" and add to that vitamin B6. A visit to a local health food store will prove helpful; remember, however, that this provides you with only one side of the debate over nutrition and eating habits.

Here is part of that story from two authorities on the subject of "stress control":

> Especially during stressful times, high levels of certain vitamins are needed to maintain properly functioning nervous and endocrine systems: These are vitamin C and the vitamins of the B complex, particularly vitamin B-1 (thiamine), B-2 (riboflavin), niacin, B-5 (pantothenic acid), B-6 (pyridoxine hydrochloride), and choline. These B-complex vitamins are important components of the stress response in that deficiencies of vitamins B-1, B-5, and B-6 can lead to anxiety reactions, depression, insomnia, and cardiovascular weaknesses, while vitamins B-2 and niacin deficiencies have been known to cause stomach irritability and muscle weakness. Their depletion lowers your tolerance to, and ability to cope with, stressors.
>
> Vitamins also play important roles in the actual mechanics of the stress response. Vitamins B-1, B-2, and niacin are used up at far greater rates during the stress response because of their roles in carbohydrate metabolism and gluconeogenesis (the process whereby the body forms glucose for more energy). . . . Furthermore, vitamins B-5, C, and choline are necessary elements in the producing of adrenal hormones secreted during the stress response. Therefore, excessive stress over prolonged periods of time will deplete these vitamins and render you highly prone to the stress-predisposing factors and side effects caused by B-complex deficiencies.
>
> A major dietary component implicated in the depletion of the necessary B-complex vitamins is refined white sugar. Sugar—and therefore sugar products such as cakes, pies, cookies, and candy—is a good source of energy but has no other redeeming feature. In order for sugar to be utilized for energy, however, the body must have B-complex vitamins. Most foods that need these vitamins for their metabolism do contain the necessary vitamins, but since sugar contains none of them, it must "borrow" the vitamins from other food sources. This creates a B-complex debt in the body. If this borrowing occurs frequently and if the body does not have sufficient sources of B vitamins from nutritious foods or supplements, the result is a B-vitamin deficiency, and symptoms such as anxiety, irritability, and general nervousness will appear. This vitamin depletion may be exacerbated by stress

because of their increased utilization in the production of stress hormones.[1]

In nutrition, as in everything else for the Christian, "Let your moderation be known to all men" (Phil. 4:5). Study the field, eat wisely, and trust God to give you a long and healthful life.

2. GET REGULAR PHYSICAL EXERCISE

I really believe in physical fitness. But like everything else in life, it must be pursued in moderation. To some people physical fitness is a god.

The human body is a living machine that will malfunction if not cared for properly. The Bible commands men to "earn their bread by the sweat of their face" (Gen. 3:19). Our sedentary lifestyle is not healthful. We need to work our bodies, respiratory and cardiovascular systems, and muscles. This is notably true for men (who have a shorter life-expectancy than women), especially if they are Type A and at the age of highest vulnerability to heart attacks (generally 45 to 60) and if they face on-going pressures. The man who exercises vigorously 20 to 30 minutes a day, four or five days a week, will not only be more fit, but will help to keep his weight down, feel better about himself, and improve his outlook on life.

I first observed that a parallel exists between vigorous exercise and mental health when I was in the air force. Many men suffering from battle fatigue as a result of fifty combat missions over Europe were still obsessed with a desire to go to officer candidate school. The intense, ninety-day physical fitness training program had an amazing influence on their mental attitude and restoration of emotional control. Through the years I have observed that physical therapy has had a more effective influence on the depressed than electrotherapy, drug therapy, or psychotherapy. I'm convinced that most depressed people can measurably improve through a combination of physical and spiritual therapy.

Keith W. Sehnert says of vigorous exercise in men:

> One of the first documented studies about the mental-health value of exercise was done at the University of Wisconsin. John Greist, a psychiatrist, did a study in 1976 which showed that

---

[1]Girdano and Everly, *Controlling Stress and Tension*, 91–92.

jogging was a better treatment for depression than psycho-therapy. In a pilot study eight clinically depressed patients participated in a 10-week running program. Six of them were cured of their depression. Greist noted that such a "cure rate" of 75 percent was substantially better than the recovery rate for similar patients treated with the traditional psychotherapy he and his staff offered.

In that study the eight patients walked and ran both alone and in groups from two to seven times a week. Most of them recovered from their depression after the first three weeks of the program and maintained their recovery with regular exercise. Patients were interviewed by computer every two weeks. By using this method the data about their health was collected without the injection of a possibly biased human interviewer. In 1978 Dr. Greist and his team of psychiatrists and psychologists expanded the study to another 28 depressed patients and found that for most of them 30 to 45 minutes of jogging three times a week was at least as effective as talk therapy.

Since then other psychiatrists, such as Robert S. Brown of the University of Virginia, Charlottesville, and Ronald M. Lawrence of the University of California in Los Angeles, also found that exercise worked better than pills in controlling depression.

Dr. Lawrence, founder and president of the American Medical Jogger's Association, an organization with more than 3000 members, told *Time* magazine: "Man was meant to be a moving animal, but he's become sedentary. Distance running can bring us back to the basic of what we're here for."

Thaddeus Kostrubala, M.D., a psychiatrist, marathoner, and author of *The Joy of Running*, has developed an unusual method of psychotherapy for his patients. He does psychotherapy while jogging alongside them and has trained "running therapists" to treat depression, drug addiction, and schizophrenia. Kostrubala notes, "I think this is a new and powerful way of reaching the unconscious. . . . I have talked to many runners—runners who run long, medium and short distances—and I have come to the conclusion that running is a form of natural psychotherapy."

Though there is no hard evidence yet, some researchers believe that running cures mental problems by changing chemicals in the body. A Purdue University professor of physical education, A. H. Ismail, recently reported "significant relationships" between changes in hormone levels of joggers and improvements in emotional stability. Skeptics of such reports say that the out-of-shape professors he studied at Purdue felt better simply because they got away from their desks. Ismail still sticks to his theory that exercise produces chemical changes. . . .

Whatever the researchers prove and the skeptics seek to disprove, several things are apparent. Exercise is helpful for many, including me. It blows out mental cobwebs and calms everyday tension.[2]

Jogging is not the only method of physical exercise that will help to relieve the pressures of life. But it is popular right now and seems to provide all the requirements of vigorous heart palpitation and stimulation for a long period within a reasonable time frame. I used to golf once a week, but the trip to the golf course and the trek over eighteen holes took more time than my five-day-a-week jog—and jogging must be twenty times more beneficial than eighteen holes of golf. The latter will take your mind off your troubles, relax your tensions (unless you're a duffer), and let you enjoy clean air and nature, but it doesn't exercise your respiratory and cardiovascular systems long enough to be significantly helpful.

Fred Kasch, former head of the physical education department at the San Diego State University graduate school, has trained hundreds of physical fitness teachers around the country. He explained to me that it takes eight to ten minutes to bring the heart and respiratory systems up to a safe pressure. To get the best value out of the program, one must keep it going for about ten to fifteen more minutes. In layman's terms, such activity cleans out the blood vessels, rejuvenates the blood cells and tissue, and possibly tones up the body's vital organs. We have already seen that ACTH is profitable in reasonable doses. It is just possible that jogging activates enough ACTH to tone the inward parts somewhat similar to the way exercise tones the muscles.

One personal illustration offering evidence that exercise is worthwhile occurred when I stepped into a shop in the hotel I stayed in on the "banquet tour." I had just called the office for my dismal financial report, and we were anticipating an endless number of future banquets. On the counter an electric gadget gave a computer readout of one's pulse rate. The card said: "50-60 super athlete, 60-70 jogger, 70-80 out of shape, 90-100 see your doctor." Putting my finger in the slot, I was elated to see a read-out of 54 in spite of all the real pressures I was experiencing. Maybe this will help you understand why I am such a

---

[2]Sehnert, *Stress/Unstress*, 173–75.

jogging enthusiast. I want to serve my Lord and enjoy marriage for many more years. I am convinced that jogging is one way to ensure meeting those goals.

SUGGESTIONS FOR JOGGERS

I would encourage you to begin a jogging program immediately, because I am confident it will benefit you greatly. But be sure to follow some basic rules.

Have a physical checkup with your doctor. Some people should not jog due to physical conditions, and your doctor is qualified to advise you on this. However, some doctors seem less objective about jogging than about nutrition. For instance, sedentary doctors often find fault with jogging. Choose a doctor who is himself physically fit and ask his advice.

Buy a good pair of shoes. An expensive sweatsuit or fancy shirt and trunks are not prerequisites for jogging, but you really do need good shoes. Properly protected feet and ankles are essential. Doctors' bad impressions of jogging are usually created by the people they have treated for ankle, foot, achilles, and leg injuries, many of which are caused by not wearing light, well-cushioned shoes.

Start slowly. As with anything else, moderation is the key to success. If you are badly out of shape, alternate jogging fifty strides and walking fifty for a half-mile. Each day increase your jogging by ten strides, but keep your walking the same. After the first week add a quarter-mile and gradually drop your walking. Then add one lap (quarter-mile) a week until you are up to the level you desire. Eventually it will take you fifteen to twenty-two minutes to do two miles, twenty-four to thirty minutes for three miles. Don't rush it; let your body find its natural rhythm. You are not competing for the Olympics, but rather trying to improve your physical fitness and relieve your pressures.

Don't jog on the street. The best place to jog is a high school or college running track. (You paid for it as a taxpayer; why not use it?) But don't jog on the highway. The pounding of your feet on the pavement is harmful. And there is the hazard of vehicular traffic. A minister friend in San Diego was just finishing a sixteen-mile jog when he was struck by a coed's car as she was

hurrying to a college class. Suffering brain damage, he perse-
vered through years of superhuman effort on his part, and contrary to the expectations of his doctors, he now serves his
former church as the minister of visitation. He is classified
"permanently disabled" by the state, for he has both speech
and equilibrium difficulties. I hope you will avoid his experience by confining your jogging to a track.

Don't brag about jogging. Your nonjogging friends may resent your progress and commitment, for you will be a threat to
their sedentary lifestyle. Discuss it at your risk. Yet all joggers
seem prone to talk about it. (I even worked it into this book.)
While jogging may help us to relieve our pressures, the very
mention of it heaps more pressure on our physically unfit
friends. So even if you can't maintain complete silence, at least
restrain your enthusiasm or soon your friendships will be limited to a small circle of joggers. Remember, we are still a
minority—but we're gaining on them.

3. KEEP YOUR WEIGHT DOWN

I was born fat (11 lbs. 8 oz.) and remained fat for the first
twenty-five years of my life. I hated it! From ages eighteen to
twenty I kept my weight reasonably in check through army
physical fitness and athletic programs. From ages twenty-one to
twenty-four I played every sport I could in college and reached
170 pounds. While I was serving as a pastor in Minneapolis, the
granary capital of the world, I let my weight rise again. Then it
happened at 190 pounds: I bent over to pick up a dead battery
in fourteen-degrees-below-zero weather when the seam in the
seat of my pants ripped. I responded either to the cold wind
against my bare legs or to my heavenly Father saying, "Son, it's
time to go on a diet!" Two days later I visited a doctor and
began an endless number of diets. Through the years I have lost
well over 1,200 pounds! I am an authority on losing—and
gaining—weight.

No one hates obesity more than the obese. Medical science
indicates that some people have a higher rate of metabolism
than others; consequently two people may eat the same foods,
and one will gain but the other will not. Some people also have
a greater appetite than others. Regardless of individual differ-

ences, obesity will intensify pressure. Not only will it make you tend to dislike yourself, which increases pressure greatly, but it will exhaust your energy and limit your spontaneity and freedom to use your natural creativity. Unfinished work will heighten your pressures. Most of all, depending on the amount of excess weight you carry, the added load on your entire system will increase your pressure in proportion to the degree that you are over your normal weight.

Because being overweight is such a major problem today, I will suggest some simple rules I have used to bring myself under control. Keeping weight down is still a struggle but I win most of the time.

See your doctor. If you are more than ten pounds overweight, do not devise your own reduction program. There are many effective programs available from the medical profession, and there is no need to create one by yourself.

Do not eat sweets, and limit your carbohydrates. Many obese people are "sweetaholics." I find I simply cannot control my consumption of sweets by any other means than total abstinence.

Cut down on calories. Breads, potatoes, dressings, beef, and many other foods have high caloric content.

Eat three meals a day. Don't snack between meals, and don't ingest food after 7:00 P.M. Sleep burns up few calories. Many people go to bed on full stomachs and gain weight during the night.

Take vitamin supplements when you diet.

Follow your doctor's orders.

Ask God's special help with this problem.

Weigh yourself every day. If you gain weight, adjust your eating accordingly.

4. AVOID DRUGS AND ALCOHOL

Drugs—and not always medically prescribed drugs—are the most common method of relieving pressure today. This is especially true if we include alcohol, which in reasonable assessment is a drug. "Hard drugs"—those beyond alcohol—all offer only temporary relief and eventually produce greater pressure. More than 50 percent of our highway accidents today are drug- and alcohol-related. The driver who has sought relief from his pressures through drinking or drug use only multiplies them if he is involved in a traffic accident or arrested by law enforcement officers.

Christians should never use drugs or alcohol as a pressure release. The Bible teaches clearly that our minds are to be controlled by the Holy Spirit rather than any inanimate substance (Eph. 5:18).

5. KEEP YOUR BACK TUNED UP

Another effective way to relieve your pressure is exercise that keeps your back flexible. You have undoubtedly noticed that tension builds up at the base of your skull, across your shoulders, or even in the lower regions of your back. This is often due to muscular tensions produced by pressure; it is accelerated by the lack of exercise of a sedentary way of life.

Your spine is the only joint system in the body that can move five different ways: Forward, backward, right, left, or twisting. Loss of flexibility in the back can pinch nerves, causing nutritional starvation to vital parts of the body and needlessly increasing pressure. The older we get, the more rigid our back becomes. This is why older people are likely to complain more of headaches or backaches. Fortunately it is not difficult to keep the spine in a flexible condition. Examine the following exercises designed by experts to maintain the spine's flexibility and improve the tone of those muscles that keep the vertebrae in place.

This exercise brings two results. It relaxes the lower back muscles and vertebrae, and it tones up the lower stomach muscles. As we grow older, these tend to relax, and we develop an unsightly paunch that can throw the body out of balance.

Lying on the floor face down, you should place your hands parallel with your chest and raise your upper body as far back as possible. Holding yourself in that position, raise and lower your head as shown by the dotted lines.

Start by lying flat on your back; rock your legs back until you create a rocking motion. Do not go too high up on your neck, but rock slowly back and forth, with your knees bent, ten times. Increase the number by one each day.

A nightly ritual of these simple exercises will relax you and improve your sleep, an indicator of relief from pressure.

6. ENJOY A NORMAL MARRIED SEX LIFE

One of the benefits of marriage is the normal and frequent release of the sex drive with one's partner. God has made us sexual beings, but only in recent years have we Christians been willing to face that fact. It is hoped that our book *The Act of Marriage* has been helpful.

The Bible clearly states that sexual expression is *only* for married people. Repeatedly singles ask me, "What are we supposed to do with our sexual pressures"? I answer, "Get married or seek God's grace for their control." No one has ever destroyed himself by sexual abstinence. God's standard of morality has not changed, and we dare not transgress it.

The sex drive can be cultivated by use, but is decreased (though not eliminated) by disuse. Consequently there is an increased demand for sexual release in marriage. As we noted earlier, the average frequency of sexual relations for most married couples is two or three times a week. Because it offers a therapeutically beneficial relief from pressure, I suggest that a loving mate be sensitive to the partner's needs, and when one observes the pressures of life building up, try to engage the partner in the act of marriage. It won't solve a mate's problems, but it will make him or her more fit to live with.

7. MEET GOD IN HIS WORD DAILY AND TALK TO HIM EACH DAY

Years ago I learned with Job that I was as dependent on the Word of God each day for my spiritual nutrition as I was on mealtimes for my physical food. That is even more important during times of pressure. Human beings have spiritual resources this world knows very little about and consequently cannot cultivate. I am convinced that Christians can endure much more pressure than their non-Christian friends. The Holy Spirit strengthens their natural weaknesses, and the Word of God fortifies the inner spiritual man. Sometimes the Bible calls this spiritual nature "the new man" (e.g., Eph. 4:24; Col 3:10). Many are the challenges in God's Word to "put on the new man," "building up yourselves in your most holy faith," "be transformed by the renewing of your mind." How do we strengthen our inner spiritual man? By renewing our mind daily in the Word of God (Rom. 12:2).

I found that when I had fallen beneath the load of my greatest pressure, I didn't *feel* like reading the Word of God each day. But that's when I needed it most. We don't always eat because we *feel* like it, but because we need to. I can testify to the benefits gained by letting my heavenly Father talk to me on a daily basis whether or not I thought I needed it.

Reading the Word of God serves two useful purposes: (1) It strengthens our inner spiritual nature, and (2) it is used by God to put a light at the end of our tunnel. More will be said on this in chapter 12. In addition to God's talking to us daily, we need to talk to Him. Conversation is a two-way process: God ministering to us through His Word, and the believer addressing Him in prayer. Everyone needs to set aside some portion of his day for this two-way spiritual communication, from ten minutes to an hour or even more. Some of your best-quality thought time belongs to God. And like all our dealings with Him, we become the richer for it.

JOGGING AND PRAYER

Long before I entered the pressure mill in 1982 I had developed a most enjoyable spiritual habit that became a tremendous tonic to my soul these past few months. You may think it strange if you are a closet pray-er, but I suspect that an activist like Paul would understand, for he "prayed without ceasing." Using the solitude of the running track, I spend the entire time talking with God. Here's my routine:

I rise early, drink a cup of (unhealthy) coffee, and read one to four chapters in God's Word. I find three or four key thoughts God will use to speak to me and then drive to the high school track.

I start jogging and worship the Lord. For the first four laps I just praise and thank God for who He is, what He means to me, and what He has done for me. Starting with lap 5, I pray for the items on my "A" list; by laps 7 and 8 I'm ready for the "B" and "C" lists. The last four laps are spent discussing my day with God, planning its activities, mentally penning a letter or two, or planning an article or writing assignment. Anything that concerns me becomes part of my conversation. After all, my heavenly Father tells me that He is interested in every detail of my existence.

By the time I return home, I feel great! My body is responding to the exhilaration of jogging, and my heart is full from my time with God. I can't always determine which forms the source of greatest joy. But I do know this is a great way to live—particularly when I'm under pressure.

CHAPTER 12

Hidden Resources

Almost everyone knows that the Bible was written to help people go to heaven when they die. But many folks do not realize that it was also written to guide them while they live here on earth. Yet it provides vital resources to cope with both the normal pressures of life and those giant pressures that sooner or later come into every life, especially those that threaten to engulf us.

At times like this you need the Bible. That is why a loving God has given it to us. Both the Old and New Testaments abound with such expressions as—

"Be not afraid."

"Fret not."

"Trust in the Lord."

"Let not your heart be troubled."

"Be anxious [worried] over nothing."

But don't expect to *want* to read the Bible when you are discouraged due to pressure. I didn't, and I've read and studied the Bible for years. Instead, I was resentful and didn't want to seek help from the Scriptures; I preferred to wallow in my self-pity. But I read God's Word anyway. Like eating when my system is upset, I knew it was good for me. Consider this sage advice:

> Why are you downcast, O my soul?
> Why so disturbed within me?

> Put your hope in God,
> for I will yet praise him,
> my Savior and my God.
> (Ps. 42:11, NIV)

Do you think you are the only person who has ever become depressed or discouraged due to pressure? Do you consider yourself the only one who felt like quitting? Of course not. The Bible was written to people just like you and me, offering both instruction and hope in the most trying of times. My story illustrates this truth.

After ten months of prayer, planning, promotion, thirty-five fund-raising banquets, and completion of the first thirteen weeks of television production, we were ready to begin telecasts. I will never forget the moment. Something said, "Wait until January." We talked about it and decided there was no time like the present to act.

Our first programs were aired on twenty stations around the country, but on October 1, I knew we were in trouble. A careful study of our financial report showed that we had exhausted all our resources and were losing money at the rate of $31,000 a month. Our accountant for Family Life Seminars, who is also our personal accountant, chose that same day to inform me that my previous accountant had made some serious errors and we must file a correction to our last three years' personal income taxes, making an additional payment that totaled 1½ years' back taxes.

When I attended church on the fourth Sunday in October, I went because it was Sunday, not because I felt like going. Everyone greeted us warmly, and many exclaimed, "We just love your new TV show!" Then they would ask, "How is everything going?" I resented the question. I had been their pastor for twenty-five years, and I found that these people whom I loved were much more confident of our eventual success than I was. But that morning I heard the perfect message. Pastor David Jeremiah, my successor, shared how God gives testing to try us, not to break us. Then he told about the need to see a light at the end of the tunnel. All I could think of was $31,000 X 12 months, or an annual loss of $393,000. Pastor David, who has since launched an excellent TV ministry in the San Diego area, is himself, I am sure, learning these same lessons. But in that message he pointed out that I had been looking in the wrong place for hope. A financial statement rarely offers hope; the Word of God always does.

Then, one year and 125 banquets later, we were on forty-two stations and five cable networks, ministering to more than one million families a week. Our operating loss was down to only $7,000 a month. At that rate another year would find us in the black, it was hoped. But operating in the black isn't nearly as important as the fact that I can now say in the midst of very distressing circumstances that God is able to supply all our needs, and His Word keeps the light shining at the end of the tunnel.

During the days of greatest pressure, I found the Word of God to be everything I had taught that it was during my years as a pastor. Each morning I would arise early (although I am not by nature an early riser) and read the Scriptures until I found some specific blessing for my soul. The following are some that I found particularly helpful. I include these at the close of this book, because they are as appropriate for us today as for those people to whom they were written in the first century. They will help you just as they did me.

OUR LORD'S MESSAGE OF HOPE

The Lord Jesus knows all about us, especially our penchant for worry, fretfulness, and anxiety. But He left some magnificent antidotes:

"Do not let your hearts be troubled. Trust in God; trust also in me" (John 14:1, NIV).

"Therefore I tell you, do not worry about your life, what you will eat or drink; or about your body, what you will wear. Is not life more important than food, and the body more important than clothes? Look at the birds of the air; they do not sow or reap or store away in barns, and yet your heavenly Father feeds them. Are you not much more valuable than they? Who of you by worrying can add a single hour to his life?" (Matt. 6:25–27, NIV).

"But seek first his kingdom and his righteousness, and all these things will be given to you as well. Therefore do not worry about tomorrow, for tomorrow will worry about itself. Each day has enough trouble of its own" (Matt. 6:33–34, NIV).

"*Ask* and it will be given to you; *seek* and you will find; *knock* and the door will be opened to you" (Matt. 7:7, NIV).

"If you, then, though you are evil, know how to give good gifts to your children, *how much more* will your Father in heaven give good gifts to those who ask him!" (Matt. 7:11, NIV).

He replied, "You of little faith, *why are you so afraid?*" Then he got up and rebuked the winds and the waves, and it was completely calm (Matt. 8:26,, NIV).

"Come to me, all you who are weary and burdened, and I will give you rest. Take my yoke upon you and learn from me, for I am gentle and humble in heart, and you will find rest for your souls. For my yoke is easy and my burden is light" (Matt. 11:28–30, NIV).

"*I will not leave you as orphans;* I will come to you" (John 14:18, NIV).

"Peace I leave with you; my peace I give you. I do not give to you as the world gives. *Do not let your hearts be troubled* and do not be afraid" (John 14:27, NIV).

"I have told you these things, so that in me you may have peace. In this world you will have trouble. But *take heart!* I have overcome the world" (John 16:33, NIV).

THE APOSTLE PAUL

It has long been a fascination to me that the apostle Paul, the most successful and productive Christian in the history of the church, also suffered more than any others we have on record. He lived through more beatings, shipwrecks, imprisonments, and destitution than any other, yet he remained faithful. At the end he announced "I kept the faith, I *finished* the course" (see 2 Tim. 4:6).

God used Paul to pen many encouraging messages that are helpful to us as we endure trials. Consider some of these promises from the man who said, "Therefore, since through God's mercy we have this ministry, we do not lose heart" (2 Cor. 4:1, NIV).

We are hard pressed on every side, but not crushed;
    perplexed, but not in despair;
    persecuted, but not abandoned;
    struck down, but not destroyed. . . .
Therefore we *do not lose heart*" (2 Cor. 4:8–9, 16, NIV).

In other words, we bend, but with God's help we do not break.

Now to him who is able to do immeasurably more than all we ask or imagine, according to his power that is at work within us, to him be glory in the church and in Christ Jesus throughout all generations, for ever and ever! Amen (Eph. 3:20–21, NIV).

Do not be anxious about anything, but in everything, by prayer and petition, *with thanksgiving,* present your requests to God And the peace of God, which transcends all understanding, will guard your hearts and your minds in Christ Jesus (Phil. 4:6–7, NIV).

For I am convinced that neither death nor life, neither angels nor demons, neither the present nor the future, nor any powers, neither height nor depth, nor anything else in all creation, *will be able to separate us from the love of God* that is in Christ Jesus our Lord (Rom. 8:38–39, NIV).

I am not saying this because I am in need, for I have learned to be content whatever the circumstances. I know what it is to be in need, and I know what it is to have plenty. *I have learned the secret of being content* in any and every situation, whether well fed or hungry, whether living in plenty or in want. I can do everything through Him who gives me strength (Phil. 4:11–13, NIV).

Do not get drunk on wine, which leads to debauchery. Instead, be filled with the Spirit. Speak to one another with psalms, hymns and spiritual songs. Sing and make music in your heart to the Lord, always giving thanks to God the Father for everything, in the name of our Lord Jesus Christ (Eph. 5:18–20, NIV).

Give thanks in all circumstances, for this is God's will for you in Christ Jesus (1 Thess. 5:18, NIV).

THE BLESSINGS OF THE PSALMS

I have never been a psalm-lover. I don't mean that I didn't believe in and enjoy the Book of Psalms, but being predominantly choleric in temperament, I have preferred Proverbs. But this year's pressures have taught me to appreciate the Psalms in a new way. I was already doing everything Proverbs had to say, but I needed comfort for my soul, reassurance for my mind, and joy in my heart—and I found them in the Psalms. Consider these, which are just some of my favorites:

To the LORD I cry aloud,
  and he answers me from his holy hill.
I lie down and sleep;
  I wake again, because the LORD sustains me.
I will not fear the tens of thousands
  drawn up against me on every side (Ps. 3:4–6, NIV).

How long must I wrestle with my thoughts
and every day have sorrow in my heart?
How long will my enemy triumph over me? . . .
But I trust in your unfailing
love;
My heart rejoices in your salvation.
I will sing to the Lord,
for *he has been good to me* (Ps. 13:2, 5–6, NIV).

I have set the Lord always before me.
Because he is at my right hand,
I will not be shaken.

Therefore *my heart is glad* and *my tongue rejoices;*
my body also will rest secure (Ps. 16:8–9, NIV).

I love you, O Lord, my strength.

The Lord is my rock, my fortress and *my deliverer;*
my God is *my rock,* in whom I take refuge.
He is *my shield* and *the horn of my salvation,*
my stronghold.
I call to the Lord, who is worthy of praise,
and I am saved from my enemies (Ps. 18:1–3, NIV)..

I am still confident of this:
I will see the goodness of the Lord
in the land of the living (Ps. 27:13, NIV).

The Lord is my strength and my shield;
my heart trusts in him, and I am helped.
My heart leaps for joy
and *I will give thanks to him in song* (Ps. 28:7, NIV).

The righteous cry out, and the Lord hears them;
he delivers them from all their troubles.
The Lord is close to the brokenhearted
and saves those who are crushed in spirit.
A righteous man may have many troubles,
but *the Lord delivers him from them all* (Ps. 34:17–19, NIV).

Trust in the Lord and do good;
dwell in the land and enjoy safe pasture.
Delight yourself in the Lord
and he will give you the desires of your heart (Ps. 37:3–4, NIV).

Wait for the Lord
and keep his way.
He will exalt you to possess the land;
when the wicked are cut off, you will see it (Ps. 37:34, NIV).

I waited patiently for the Lord;
  he turned to me and heard my cry.
He lifted me out of the slimy pit,
  out of the mud and mire;
he set my feet on a rock
  and gave me a firm place to stand.
He put a new song in my mouth,
  a hymn of praise to our God.
Many will see and fear
  and put their trust in the Lord.

Blessed is the man
  who makes the Lord *his trust* (Ps. 40:1–4, NIV).

God is our refuge and strength,
  an ever present help in trouble.
Therefore we will not fear, though the earth give way
  and the mountains fall into the heart of the sea (Ps. 46:1–2, NIV).

Cast your cares on the Lord
  and he will sustain you;
  he will never let the righteous fall (Ps. 55:22, NIV).

My soul faints with longing for your salvation,
  but *I have put my hope in your word* (Ps. 119:81, NIV).

I have not departed from your laws,
  for you yourself have taught me.
How sweet are your promises to my taste,
  sweeter than honey to my mouth!
I gain understanding from your precepts;
  therefore I hate every wrong path.
Your word is a lamp to my feet
  and a light for my path (Ps. 119:102–105, NIV).

I lift up my eyes to the hills—
  where does my help come from?
My help comes from the Lord,
  the Maker of heaven and earth.

He will not let your foot slip—
  he who watches over you will not slumber;
indeed, he who watches over Israel
  will neither slumber nor sleep.

The Lord watches over you—
  the Lord is your shade at your right hand;
the sun will not harm you by day,
  nor the moon by night.

The Lord will keep you from all harm—
   he will watch over your life;
the Lord will watch over your coming and going
   both now and forevermore (Ps. 121, NIV).

These are only some examples. The Bible is filled with encouragement to us as God's children. When you are pressured, let God speak to you *personally* from His Word. Mark the special verses; memorize some, and review them all.[1] You will find them to be a continuing daily source of encouragement and strength, for as long as you live.

Then you will see Him face to face. Your pressures will be over, and your life will be void of war, turmoil, and fear. Until then you need to use your Bible daily as a ready release from all the pressures of life.

---

[1] *How to Study the Bible for Yourself* by Tim LaHaye (Eugene, Ore.: Harvest House, 1976), will be helpful in establishing a consistent Bible study program.

Bibliography

Biermann, June, and Barbara Toohey. *The Woman's Holistic Headache Relief Book.* Los Angeles: J. P. Tarcher, 1979.

Blaiklock, David A. *Release from Tension.* Grand Rapids: Zondervan Publishing House, 1969.

Carlson, Dwight L. *Run and Not be Weary.* Old Tappan, N.J.: Fleming H. Revell, 1974.

Collins, Gary. *You Can Profit From Stress.* Santa Ana, Calif: Vision House Publishers, 1977.

Dudley, Donald L., and Elton Welke. *How to Survive Being Alive.* New York: New American Library, 1979.

Girdano, Daniel, and George Everly. *Controlling Stress and Tension: A Holistic Approach.* Englewood Cliffs, N.J.: Prentice-Hall, 1979.

Jenson, Ron, with Chuck MacDonald. *Together We Can Deal With Life in the 80's.* San Bernardino, Calif.: Here's Life Publishers, 1982.

Keller, W. Phillip. *Taming Tension.* Grand Rapids: Baker Book House, 1979.

LaHaye, Tim. *How to Win Over Depression.* Grand Rapids: Zondervan Publishing House, 1974.

_____ . *Spirit-Controlled Temperament.* Wheaton, Ill.: Tyndale House Publishers, 1966.

_____ . *Understanding the Male Temperament.* Old Tappan, N.J.: Fleming H. Revell, 1977.

Larson, Bruce. *There's a Lot More to Health Than Not Being Sick.* Waco, Tex: Word Books, 1981.

McMillen, S. I. *None of These Diseases.* Old Tappan, N.J.: Fleming H. Revell, 1981.

McQuade, Walter, and Ann Aikman. *Stress.* New York: Bantam Books, 1974.

Morris, Barbara M. *Change Agents in the Schools.* Ellicott City, Md.: The Barbara M. Morris Report, 1979.

Osgood, Don. *Pressure Points, The Christian's Response to Stress.* Chappaqua, N.Y.: Christian Herald Books, 1978.

Perry, Charles, Jr. *Why Christians Burn Out.* Nashville: Thomas Nelson Publishers, 1982.

Schuller, Robert H. *Turning Your Stress Into Strength.* Irvine, Calif: Harvest House Publishers, 1978.

Sehnert, Keith W. *Stress/Unstress.* Minneapolis: Augsburg Publishing House, 1981.

Selye, Hans. *Stress Without Distress.* New York: New American Library, 1974.

_____. *The Stress of Life.* New York: McGraw-Hill, rev. ed., 1975.

Shealey, C. Normand. *The Pain Game.* Millbrae, Calif: Celestial Arts, 1976.

Van Alstine, George. *The Christian and the Public Schools.* Nashville: Abingdon, 1982.

Yates, Jere E. *Managing Stress—A Businessperson's Guide.* New York: AMACOM, 1979.